Praise for *Unleashing Creativity and Innovation*

"In a world of talk about innovation, Birla shows us exactly *how* it's done. He demystifies ingenuity itself with simple anecdotes and a tried, true, tangible process for entrepreneurs, intrapreneurs, and business leaders."

—Chris "Kiff" Gallagher, Jr.,
CEO and Founder, Musiciancorps.org

"I pondered over the contents of this book and realized that Madan is so right in pointing out that creativity is natural and essential to personal and organizational success. Organizations just need to create the four (MINT) conditions to tap into this natural resource and unleash their competitive edge."

—Rajiv Grover, Ph.D., Dean, Fogelman College of
Business & Economics, University of Memphis

"Madan's insight into nature's lessons on business and life was both practical and thought-provoking. This book got my creative juices flowing and reminded me of the importance of what I can learn from nature's teaching . . . if I will simply stop and pay attention."

—Ben Buffington, Chairman of the Board,
Hi-Speed Industrial Service

unleashing
creativity
and
innovation

unleashing
creativity
and
innovation

nine lessons from nature
for enterprise growth
and career success

madan birla

WILEY

Published by John Wiley & Sons, Inc., Hoboken, New Jersey.
Published simultaneously in Canada.

All images are from iStockphoto.com. Used with permission.

For general information about our other products and services, please contact our Customer Care Department within the United States at (800) 762–2974, outside the United States at (317) 572–3993 or fax (317) 572–4002.

Wiley publishes in a variety of print and electronic formats and by print-on-demand. Some material included with standard print versions of this book may not be included in e-books or in print-on-demand. If this book refers to media such as a CD or DVD that is not included in the version you purchased, you may download this material at http://booksupport.wiley.com. For more information about Wiley products, visit www.wiley.com.

Library of Congress Cataloging-in-Publication Data:

Birla, Madan.
   Unleashing creativity and innovation: nine lessons from nature for enterprise growth and career success / Madan Birla.
      p. cm.
   Includes index.
   ISBN 978–1–118–76811–2 (cloth); ISBN 978–1–118–79478–4 (ebk);
   ISBN 978–1–118–79477–7 (ebk)
      1. Creative ability in business. 2. Creative thinking. 3. New products. 4. Technological innovations. I. Title.
   HD53.B554   2014

                                                658.4′063—dc23

Printed in the United States of America

10 9 8 7 6 5 4 3 2 1

*For Shayli, Shaan, Kayan, and Rohin
Watching you grow and blossom is the
biggest joy in my life.*

CONTENTS

Preface

Your Organization's Top Needs: Creativity and Innovation

I spend a lot of time travelling the world, speaking to leaders of organizations about leading for innovation and growth. As I prepare for these engagements, I request a meeting with the chief executive officers (CEOs) to understand the challenges they are facing. This allows me to tailor my remarks to address their specific concerns. A question I always ask is, "What keeps you awake at night?"

The most common response: "To continue to grow in today's economy, we have to outthink and outperform the competition. To have a competitive edge, we must have an innovation edge. How do we do that?"

Want to Move Up? Meet Your Boss's and Organization's Top Needs

If you work in an organization, large or small, you're probably looking for ways to increase your contribution and enhance your career prospects. That's what I was searching for continually during my 30-year career at RCA and FedEx.

Thinking back about all the promotions and awards I received at both companies, they were the result of focusing on my boss's biggest problems; conceptualizing novel solutions by asking, "What if [we did this or that]"; and then leading teams to produce the innovation we needed. My goal for this book is to share proven insights and strategies to help you unleash your potential for creativity and innovation.

Most of us go to work and fulfill job responsibilities to the best of our abilities. We do the same thing day after day. This is routine and nothing extraordinary. But when I reflect on my 22 years at FedEx, I realize that both I and the teams I led played an important part in FedEx becoming the global icon it is today. The following personal incident illustrates two important points, directly related to the subject of the book.

Several years after I left FedEx, I visited the FedEx headquarters to cash in some options to buy more FedEx stock. I was in the elevator when Fred Smith, founder and CEO of FedEx, stepped in.

He asked, "Madan, how are you doing?"

"Fine, sir," I responded.

Wanting to make small talk I said, "Fred, I saw you at the Tigers (University of Memphis' basketball team) game last week."

"Yes, I go to some games," he replied.

"Fred, I need to thank you."

"For what?" he asked.

"The only thing doing well in my portfolio is FedEx stock. Everything else has been going down."

"Madan, you need to have confidence in FedEx stock. You helped design the system."

As member of the Long Range Planning Committee (LRPC) I attended four-hour meetings, chaired by Fred, every third Tuesday of the month for nine years. In these meetings we discussed innovative strategic options (what ifs) for designing the global package movement systems and operations.

"I absolutely do and that's why I'm holding on to the FedEx stock." The elevator reached the ground floor; we shook hands and walked to our respective cars in the parking lot.

Point 1: Management notices our creative contributions.

Point 2: Although I'd been gone from FedEx for several years, Fred still made it a point to recognize my contributions, exhibiting a key leadership behavior for tapping into employees' creativity and commitment. Leading by example, Fred inspired all FedEx managers to lead for innovation and growth.

WHY I STARTED STUDYING NATURE

Looking to resolve work-life balance conflicts when my kids were very young, I asked the question, "Why do we make the life choices we do?" This search to understand human nature expanded over time to studying humans, nature, and organizations—three related living systems.

I discovered that:

- All living systems are guided by some common principles and processes. For example, each living system has a need to grow. If it is not growing, it withers and dies.

- Nature is the oldest living system and is constantly and successfully adapting to an ever-changing environment. It has been solving problems for millenniums. To study and take advantage of nature's solutions there is a growing field called biomimicry. The principles and processes from nature, the oldest living system, can help other living systems—people and organizations—adapt to the changing environment and thrive.

"WHAT IFS" MEET THE PSYCHOLOGICAL NEEDS OF "MAKING A DIFFERENCE" AND "EXPERIENCING GROWTH"

The nature of all living things is to grow. If a tree is not growing, it's dead. Why do we get bored doing the same things repeatedly? Because the work has become routine and we are not being challenged and experiencing growth. We feel most alive when we are being creative, being productive, making a difference, in love, and at play.

Certainly, the paycheck (that is, the monetary rewards) allow us to make the mortgage payment, pay the car note, send our kids to college, take a vacation, and cover other living expenses. But it is the opportunity for expression and application of our creative ideas that satisfies the psychological needs of making a difference and experiencing growth.

It goes against the human spirit to spend our waking hours doing tasks with no intellectual creativity. We are meant to create, discover, understand, explore, and inquire. Machines cannot create art, will not create the next Facebook or plot the course to explore the universe, nor increase our understanding of the human experience—only humanity can achieve those ends.

—BEN, *Long Island, NY, March 6, 2011,*
commenting online on Paul Krugman's column
in the New York Times

INTRODUCTION

In this book I answer three questions I am asked regularly during my conversations with executives and professionals around the world:

- How do I unleash my creativity and innovation potential to enhance my chances for promotion?
- How can I add the most value now that I've moved into management?
- How can my business sustain enterprise growth in today's highly competitive global economy?

The book is organized in five parts to answer these questions.

- Part I discusses in detail the creative thinking process and emphasizes the critical role of creativity and innovation, both in enterprise growth and career success.
- Part II presents the four requirements for the mind to generate creative ideas. Real-world examples are used to illustrate the practical role of each requirement in creative problem solving.

- Part III discusses the seven lessons from nature to be applied in creating the four requirements. Application of each lesson is supported by in-depth conversations with innovative and successful individuals.

- Part IV presents the proven process that innovation is generation, acceptance, and implementation of creative ideas that enhance a company's value to the customer, differentiating the company from the competition. It is a three-step people process.

- Part V suggests the important role the managers' day-to-day behaviors play in facilitating the innovation process. It presents two important lessons from nature, the keys to managers successfully fulfilling their leadership roles to encourage active participation in the innovation process. Here also are in-depth conversations with innovative leaders that illustrate the real-world application of these lessons.

PART I

Creativity and Innovation

The Keys to Enterprise Growth and Career Success in the Twenty-First Century

---

Creativity is to the marketplace what water is to life: You can have one without the other, but not for very long.
—Jim Blasingame, *The Commercial Appeal*, May 21, 2012

A recent poll of 1,500 CEOs identified creativity as the No. 1 "leadership competency" of the future.
—*Newsweek*, July 19, 2010

"WHAT IF" THINKING: THE DRIVER BEHIND FEDEX'S LAUNCH AND GROWTH INTO A GLOBAL ICON

Since my book *FedEx Delivers* has been translated into Chinese, Russian, Spanish, Korean, Thai, Vietnamese, and other languages, I often am speaking to business groups around the world. The most common question I'm asked is, "How did Fred Smith build such a great company?"

After realizing that there was a growing demand for a time-definite express mode of transportation for shipping high-priority, time-sensitive cargo such as computer parts, critical documents, medicines, and electronics, Fred Smith thought, "What if there was an airline dedicated to providing overnight express service to meet this growing need?" This was the subject of a term paper he wrote while in school at Yale University.

This what if thinking gave birth to FedEx. But what helped it become a global business success story is the what if culture; that is, people across the organization continually asking what if questions.

In my first 10 years at FedEx, I led the Materials and Resource Planning function. That allowed my group to be involved in all new marketing initiatives. One simple example: Someone in marketing thought out loud, "What if we introduce a flat rate envelope, called the Overnight Letter, to make it easier for customers to ship documents?" Within six months of its introduction, FedEx was handling more than 100,000 Overnight Letters every night.

For my next nine years at FedEx, I served as a member of the Long Range Planning Committee. My group at any point in time was evaluating at least 8 to 10 strategic what ifs. Some examples included:

- What if we automate the package and document sorting in the Memphis hub to speed up processing and launch the planes earlier to ensure on-time delivery?

- What if we open up a hub in Paris, Dubai, and Greensboro to better serve our customers around the world?

- What if we change the package pickup cutoff time in a certain zip code from 4 PM to 5 PM to improve our competitive position?

A WHAT IF SUGGESTION: THE REASON BEHIND MY FIRST BIG PROMOTION

After completing my graduate work at the Illinois Institute of Technology in Chicago, I joined RCA Records' Planning and Engineering group in Indianapolis as an industrial engineer. While speaking to undergraduate students at the University of Miami I asked, "Let me see shows of hands. Who knows what an LP is?" Not a single student raised a hand. Yes, there was a time in the distant past when music came on physical products—vinyl Long Play records called LPs, as well as on 8-track tapes and cassettes.

After enrolling in RCA's record club, RCA Music Service, members received eight records or tapes for one penny.

Thereafter, every month members received a catalog containing more than 400 selections and were obligated to buy eight records or tapes over the next 12 months. RCA Music Service hired consultants to automate the manual process of picking and packing the individual orders.

I was assigned as the in-house engineer to support RCA Music Service management on this project. The consultant proposed a computer-controlled automated pick and pack system. In this concept a tote box assigned to an order traveled on a conveyor between bins of records, 8-track tapes, and cassettes installed on each side. As the tote stopped in front of the ordered selection, the computer sent a signal to drop the product in the tote.

The prototype performed well operationally, but there was a big problem: The finance department objected to the total cost, and the resulting return on investment (ROI) was projected to be below the corporate threshold. The problem: the system's price tag was driven by the number of automated product bins required to accommodate the monthly catalog offering of more than 400 selections. I analyzed the customers' order activity for the past 12 months and found that 80 percent of the activity was accounted for by 20 percent of the selections, the Pareto principle in action.

Based on this analysis, I made a proposal to Dale, the head of RCA Music Service: "What if the automated system handled the 20 percent of selections that accounted for 80 percent of customers' choices and the rest could be handled manually?" This design substantially reduced the capital requirements and brought the ROI above the required corporate threshold. Dale liked the idea, and we secured finance's approval to proceed. The following week he called me into his office to offer me a promotion to the newly created position of Manager, Warehouse Distribution Systems, reporting to him.

> If you just do what you are told to do, you will never get promoted or recognized. It is always about trying new things and making them come true.
> —*Oh Se-hoon, Mayor, Seoul, South Korea,* Newsweek, *December 15, 2008*

ENTERPRISE NEEDS INNOVATION FROM EVERYONE

In today's highly competitive global economy, business growth depends on the ability of the company to outthink and outperform the competition. Management desperately needs creative ideas to improve products, reduce costs, and better serve its customers.

Ideas drive growth. Ideas create competitive differentiation. Ideas are your key to enjoying a successful career in the twenty-first century.

> Many people believe that the way to drive innovation is to carve out a few creative people. Our view is entirely different. We need innovation from everyone.
> —*David Withman, CEO, Whirlpool, "CEOs on Managing Globally,"* Fortune *magazine*

"I LIKE THE WAY YOU THINK" STARTED RAM ON A VERY SUCCESSFUL AND FULFILLING CAREER JOURNEY

A few years ago, after a speaking tour in India, I was flying back home to Memphis. Seated next to me on this long flight from Mumbai to Atlanta was Jayant Pendharkar, global head of marketing for Tata Consulting Services (TCS), India's largest information technology services company. When he learned that I live in the United States, he asked me the purpose of my India trip.

I told him I gave "Leading for Innovation and Growth" talks at Infosys, Wipro, Indian School of Business, the Times of India, and other companies all over India as part of my book promotion tour.

He asked, "Why didn't you speak at TCS?"

I told him the talks were set up by the public relations company handling the book tour.

Jayant suggested that I should plan to speak at TCS during my next India trip. I told him, "I'm working on another book exploring career success in the business world, and part of my research involves talking to successful business executives. So, if you can arrange for me to have an hour with the CEO of TCS, then in return I'll give you 4 hours during my next India trip."

A few months after this conversation I received an e-mail from Jayant that Ram Ramadorai, CEO of TCS, would soon be in New York and available to meet with me. We scheduled a meeting at the TCS New York office.

First, I thanked Ram for taking time from his busy schedule to meet with me; then I asked him to walk me through his career journey to becoming CEO of TCS.

After receiving his Bachelor's degree in Physics from Delhi University Ram completed a Bachelor's of Engineering degree in Electronics and Telecommunications from the Indian Institute of Science, Bangalore (India) and a Master's degree in Computer Science from the University of California, Los Angles (UCLA). In 1993, Ram attended the Sloan School of Management's Senior Executive Development program.

Ram shared, "I joined TCS in 1972 as a systems analyst and programmer in their Mumbai office. In 1979 Mr. Kohli, head of TCS, asked me to go to New York. I asked him, 'What do you want me to do there?' He said, 'Ram, I like the way you think, and I'm sure you'll figure it out.'"

As they say, the rest is history. Ram's creative thinking and dedication was the key to establishing TCS in the United States at a time when information technology (IT) consulting from India was nonexistent. As a result of this successful assignment he was asked to return to India to play a bigger role at the Mumbai headquarters. He was appointed CEO of TCS in 1996. Under Ram's leadership TCS grew exponentially. With 2011 revenue of more than $10 billion, TCS is now a globally recognized leader in providing innovative information technology solutions.

As Ram did, you should build a reputation for thinking creatively—a creative problem solver. Then senior management will seek you out for greater responsibilities and promotion. During our conversation I learned that Ram and I did our primary and high schooling in New Delhi and spent lots of time in the same neighborhoods. He spoke passionately about his interests in classical music, nature, sports, people, and his morning walks along the sea in Mumbai. He is a voracious reader. His reading interests range from science and technology to sports, biographies, and music. You'll see later in the book as to how these varied personal interests and passions contribute toward becoming a creative problem solver.

Among other global organizations Ram serves on the board of MIT Sloan School of Management and recently Kuala Lumpur based budget airline AirAsia announced Ram as chairman of its India operations.

For the record, I gave 14 hours to TCS by facilitating three four-hour sessions in Kolkata, Noida, and Gurgaon and a two-hour session at the corporate headquarters in Mumbai.

I'm looking for bold ideas. I want people who are looking for a challenge. I want to have a conversation with somebody where we can have a good debate about something. I want to feel like they're going to be additive. I want people in the room who are going to tell me things I haven't thought about before.

—*Marjorie Kaplan, President, Animal Planet and Science Networks*, New York Times, *March 5, 2011*

CREATIVITY IS USING IMAGINATION TO ASK WHAT IF?

What if we make this change in our business strategy, product design, manufacturing process, distribution process, billing system, accounting system . . . ?

Creativity is the generation of novel/new ideas by:

- Connecting dots and making connections between seemingly unrelated variables.
- Imagining things in a fresh light.
- Questioning current assumptions.

We don't have to force the mind to think creatively because the nature of the mind is to think. *If the mind is healthy and growing, it will produce creative ideas.* We just have to provide the right conditions for the mind to engage in generating creative ideas. The amazing thing is that you don't even have to try very hard to be creative—it just happens naturally and automatically.

YOUR SIMPLE IDEAS ARE VALUABLE AND MUCH NEEDED

Yes, Fred Smith had the conceptual what if for starting FedEx, but it's the thousands of what ifs by employees at all levels that turned his concept into a global business success story. I know firsthand that the team of engineers and planners I worked with came up with hundreds of what ifs while designing the package sorting hubs around the world. If you asked Fred Smith what the key to FedEx's success is, he would be the first one to tell you that it's the combined extra effort, "discretionary effort"—their creativity and commitment—of FedEx employees at all levels of the organization.

In 1979 Sony introduced the Walkman and quickly became the leader in selling portable music players. Steve Jobs at Apple thought, "What if we combine the music hardware (the player) and the software (music) and also make it easy for the customer to purchase the music they want?" Yes, Jobs thought of the original concept, but it was the cumulative what ifs (creative ideas) by hundreds of employees at Apple that turned Jobs's conceptual what if into globally successful products: the iPod, iTunes, iPad, and iPhones.

Other Examples of the Mind Connecting Dots in Imaginative Ways to Solve Problems

- What if there was a video rental service similar to a health club? *Solution: Netflix*

I had a big late fee for "Apollo 13." It was six weeks late, and I owed the video store $40. I had misplaced the cassette. It was all my fault. I started thinking, "How come movie rentals don't work like a health club, where, whether you use it a lot or little, you get the same charge?"

—*Reed Hastings, CEO, Netflix*

- What if there was a card that could be used as cash? *Solution: credit card*

In 1950, Frank McNamara found himself in a restaurant with no money and came up with the idea of the Diners Club Card. The first credit card changed the nature of buying and selling throughout the world.

—Management Review, *November 1998*

- What if there was a clean, friendly, and moderately priced accommodation for a traveling family? *Solution: Holiday Inn*

When the Wilson family of Memphis went on a motoring vacation, they discovered it was not much fun to stay in motels that were either too expensive or too slovenly. So Kemmons Wilson built his own. The first Holiday Inn opened in Memphis in 1952.

—Management Review, *November 1998*

ARE COMPANIES FACING NEW COMPETITIVE CHALLENGES IN THE CURRENT BUSINESS ENVIRONMENT?

Yes, of course they are! Common challenges and changes of today include:

- Customer expectations and demands
- Technological advancements

- Global economy
- Government regulations
- Changing demographics

IS THE RATE OF CHANGE GOING TO SLOW DOWN?

No! For companies to grow in this rapidly changing business environment, the internal rate of change must exceed the external rate of change. Innovation is imperative if companies want to grow. This presents an ideal opportunity for you to make creative contributions toward helping your organization grow.

> Creativity in any large organization does not come from one individual, the celebrity CEO. That stuff's B.S. Creativity in an organization starts where the action is—either in the laboratory, or in R&D sites, at a customer place, in manufacturing.
> —*Sam Palmisano, CEO, IBM, BW Online, March 17, 2003*

PART II

The Four Requirements for the Mind to Generate Creative Ideas

Hasbro's key skill is our ability to design and make great games and toys. We develop intellectual property, so it's important to develop the creativity and skills of our people.

—Al Verrecchia, CEO, Hasbro Inc.

CREATIVITY IN THE BUSINESS WORLD

Creativity is the process of generating ideas—ideas that will help the enterprise become more competitive in the marketplace. Business creativity means generating ideas that improve customer experience, create new products, increase revenue/market share, or improve efficiency.

Quarterly earnings are the score. Unique processes, value propositions, capabilities, customer experiences, and market positioning—all products of creative and innovative thinking—determine the score.

WHAT IF WE TYPED USING ONLY OUR THUMBS? THE BIRTH OF THE BLACKBERRY

In the mid-1990s, Research in Motion (RIM) was a modestly successful pager company. But founder Mike Lazaridis saw potential in the idea of a portable email device. He began to consider what it might look like, what it could do. He imagined something much smaller than a laptop but easier to type on than a phone. Laptops were already shrinking and bumping up against limitations on how small a QWERTY keyboard could reasonably get. Lazaridis stepped back to consider how a much tinier keyboard could be feasible—and he achieved a leap of logic: What if we typed using only our thumbs? He soon had a prototype and concrete feedback from it.

—*Roger L. Martin and Jennifer Riel*, Bloomberg Businessweek, *January 25, 2010*

ONGOING CREATIVITY AND INNOVATION: A MUST FOR SUSTAINING MARKET LEADERSHIP

With this innovation BlackBerry created the market for mobile e-mail and enjoyed a leading market share. However, the rate of change in the larger environment in which BlackBerry competes was accelerating, and BlackBerry's internal rate of change (innovation) did not keep pace with the external rate of change. As a result BlackBerry has lost significant market share to other, more innovative companies, particularly Apple and Samsung.

INNOVATION: CONNECTING DOTS FROM DISPARATE FIELDS

In the history of business more innovations have come from borrowing and combining than from invention.

- Henry Ford has been recorded saying, "I invented nothing new. I simply assembled into a car the discoveries of other men behind whom were centuries of work." Ford got the idea of a car assembly line by watching a stockyard operation at a train station. In his imagination he could a see a relationship between car manufacturing and the stockyard operation.

- Gutenberg used his knowledge of the screw press used for making wine as the basis for designing a printing press, by imaginatively connecting dots from two completely different fields.

Groundbreaking new ideas are the results of someone asking, "What if we combine this one existing idea/product with another existing idea/product to solve a problem?" How many years did both the suitcase and wheels exist before someone said, "What if we put wheels on the suitcases to make them easier to take with us?"

GENERATING (MINTING) IDEAS

Generating new ideas is a process of the mind connecting "dots" (knowledge) in imaginative ways by asking what if? The mind requires the following four conditions to engage in the creative thinking process:

More Dots (Knowledge Base)	Imagination (To connect dots)	Nominal Stress (Creative Tension)	Time (To Think)

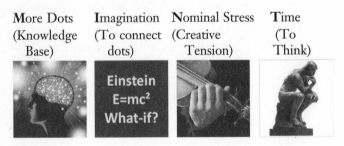

Webster's Dictionary

Mint v. To coin, to invent; to forge; to fabricate
(The mind fabricates ideas from knowledge, the raw material it has available.)

Mint n. A source of abundant supply

(The mind with its imagination capability has an unlimited capacity for generating ideas.)

The first requirement for minting or forging ideas is to gather the required raw material: more dots.

M STANDS FOR MORE DOTS: EXPANDED KNOWLEDGE BASE

Learning, curiosity, education, and creativity are
part of the same constellation.
—*RPG, Redwood City, CA, August 23, 2011,
commenting online*, New York Times

Creativity is about connecting the dots. The more dots you have to work with, the more combinations available to help generate new ideas. Curiosity generates more knowledge (dots), which precedes creativity. Creative people always ask why and continuously question the assumptions behind the existing business models, product designs, and business processes. These assumptions may have been valid 5 or 10 years ago when the process or product was initially designed, but the world and technology have changed significantly since then.

She was enormously curious. She wanted
to know why we were doing some things at the

time, and she was always prepared in a way that
I thought was refreshing.

*—A senior Xerox executive talking about Ursula Burns,
Xerox CEO*, New York Times, *February 21, 2010*

LEONARDO DA VINCI: A CLASSIC EXAMPLE OF EXPANDED KNOWLEDGE BASE

In his August 4, 2010, *New York Times* column, Tom Friedman quoted Marc Tucker, the president of the National Center on Education and the Economy, telling him, "One thing we know about creativity is that it typically occurs when people who have mastered two or more quite different fields use the framework in one to think afresh about the other. Intuitively, you know this is true. Leonardo da Vinci was a great artist, scientist, and inventor, and each specialty nourished the other. He was a great lateral thinker. But if you spend your whole life in one silo, you will never have either the knowledge or mental agility to do synthesis, connect the dots, which is usually where the next great breakthrough is found."

I STANDS FOR IMAGINATION

Imagination is the right brain asking what if by connecting dots in imaginative ways, as reflected by Einstein's quote, "Imagination is more important than knowledge. Knowledge is limited. Imagination encircles the world." The creative power of our imagination stirs the growing knowledge base (more dots) into action.

At FedEx, all offices had a Panaboard, a white board linked to a computer so that it could capture and save what is written on the board. Whenever someone came to my office to discuss a problem, the tendency was to start writing on the Panaboard the steps we needed to take to solve the problem. I observed that I was not alone in jumping into how to mode. It is a standard operating procedure for all left-brain analytical folks. Creative problem solving requires the use of both sides of our brain, the analytical and rational left and the imaginative and intuitive right. But creative thinking starts in the right brain. Using their imagination, creative problem solvers explore what ifs before locking into how to.

An imaginative mind borrows a technology or processes from one field and uses it to solve an unrelated problem in another field.

FROM NASCAR PIT TO SCALLOPED POTATO PRODUCTION

For switching over from scalloped to au gratin potatoes you have to stop the line, do some cleanups, in some cases change the dimensions of the parts on the line . . . In a couple of these plants (at General Mills) the changeover could take as long as 12 hours, and so you'd be down and wouldn't be getting the production during that time. Implementing ideas spurred by a team visiting NASCAR pit procedures, some plants managed to reduce downtime to as little as 20 minutes.

—World Traveler Magazine, *March 2002*

Just because you have not exercised your imagination lately does not mean that you have lost this wonderful capability. It's waiting to be unleashed. Remind yourself and trust that creativity is in fact the true nature you were born with.

N STANDS FOR NOMINAL STRESS (CREATIVE TENSION)

For the violin string to produce the right tone it needs the right amount of stress. Under too much tension the string snaps; without any tension, it does not produce any music.

Similarly the mind needs creative tension. Creative tension is the gap between where we are and where we want to be.

How many times have you come out of the shower with a solution to a problem that had been on your mind? You had a good night's sleep and were relaxed in general. In this state the neurons were playing around and making new connections to resolve the tension. To make new connections the mind needs to be in a playful mode.

An overly stressed mind is not in a creative mode. When under stress the neurons take the path of least resistance: the known pathways. When facing change, the response then becomes, "This is the way we've always done things around here." An overly stressed mind says, "Don't talk to me about the future. Let me get through today."

George Ballas was experiencing creative tension from trying to mow his tree-packed lawn. To solve this problem he created a prototype Weed Eater from a tin can and fishing wire.

The role of leaders is to set specific goals for improving business processes, cost structure, customer experience, and so on, the goal being a stretch, that is, far enough to require greater effort but not too far away to be unattainable. This creates the required creative tension and gets the creative problem-solving journey started.

Example: You're in a meeting and the boss at the beginning of the meeting gives a general talk about the competitive environment or the global economy and states that he wants everyone to think creatively and be innovative. Everyone sitting around the table is feeling stressed and wondering, "What does he mean, 'be creative and innovative'?" This reaction occurs because there is no specific improvement target for the activity/function that you can do something about.

Netflix, the movie rental company, set a goal of improving the movie recommendations made by its internal software by at least 10 percent, as measured by predicted-versus-actual one-through-five star ratings provided by customers, and offered a $1 million prize to the winner. This provided the creative tension to engage creative minds all over the world in addressing this challenge.

T STANDS FOR TIME

Creative problem solving requires time to engage the mind in exploring what if before locking into how to. Also, it takes time to develop a raw creative idea and get it ready for implementation.

If you're constantly running from one meeting to another, where is the time to think? Your busy calendar must reflect a balance between doing and thinking by scheduling some quiet time to just think. For example, Intuit, an accounting and financial software provider, gives its employees 10 percent of their hours as unstructured time, time to think creatively for improving Intuit products and services.

Another well-proven avenue is taking time to ask why— to question current assumptions. Hertz, Avis, and other large companies assumed that people rent cars when they travel. The Enterprise rental car company team questioned that assumption by observing that people also need cars when their vehicle is being repaired. They also often need cars when having normal maintenance done at the dealership. Enterprise set up a system to deliver cars to customers at home, dealers, or repair shops. This allowed them to develop a very successful business in an untapped market segment.

From time to time, I like to take a "thinking day."
These are pre-scheduled, uninterrupted times to
step away from the chaos, zero-base my time, and
refocus on the issues that are most important.
—*John Donahoe, CEO, eBay, LinkedIn post, July 15, 2013*

So, to recap:

- Gathering raw material, expanding your knowledge base, takes time.

- Processing the raw material into new products (that is, making new connections) requires time.

- All creative ideas when first generated are raw. They need to be developed to get them ready for implementation. This last important step in the three-step innovation process also needs time.

PART III

Seven *Unleashing Creativity* Lessons from Nature for Creating the Requirements

---

Creative potential is always alive and vital within us. We break it open and release it by letting go of limiting beliefs about who we are and by realizing what we are capable of becoming. The magnificence that resides within the seed of what becomes a giant Sequoia tree is the same magnificence that also indwells us.

—Kathy Juline, *Science of Mind*, December 2010

NATURE: A RICH RESOURCE FOR UNDERSTANDING OURSELVES

All ideas—including creative ideas—originate in our mind. By better understanding how our minds work, we can use this knowledge to unleash our natural creative potential. One avenue for better understanding our mind—our own nature—is to study Mother Nature, that is, the principles at work in nature at large.

Meaning, moods, the whole scale of our inner experience, finds in nature "the correspondences" through which we may know our boundless selves.

—*Kathleen Raine, quoted by Sarah Ban Breathnach in, 'Simple Abundance'*

I love to think of nature as an unlimited broadcasting station, through which God speaks to us every hour, if we only tune in.

—*George Washington Carver*

Nature is a teacher with great wisdom to impart; our job is not to subdue or protect ourselves from it, but to enjoy its beauty and learn what we can of its secrets.

—*Barry Ebert*, Science of Mind, *May 2009*

Never does nature say one thing and wisdom another.

—*Juvenal*, Satires

Nature: A Fertile Environment for Creative Thinking

The innovative application of technology has been the key to FedEx becoming a global leader in the logistics industry. Rob Carter, FedEx's chief information officer (CIO), is responsible for setting the technology direction. *Fast Company* magazine named Rob number 18 on their list of "The 100 Most Creative People in Business" in 2010. He is a multiple recipient of the Chief of the Year award from *Info Week* and *CIO* magazines.

> For many years, I've enjoyed the tranquility of the Smokey Mountains. It's a place that quiets my soul while energizing me at the same time.
>
> I've taken my team there several times and have seen an interesting pattern. We arrive full of cares and problems we are currently dealing with. As we dive into solving "world hunger," I always make sure we have lots of time to hike and enjoy the setting and majesty of the ancient mountains.
>
> Each time, I've found the "problems" become so much more clear and solutions emerge—not as we strain to solve them in a cramped conference room, but rather as we walk down the path and listen to the leaves and streams whisper.
>
> —*Rob Carter, CIO, FedEx*

> As you sit on the hillside, or lie prone under the trees of the forest, or sprawl wet-legged by a mountain stream, the great door that does not look like a door, opens.
>
> —*Stephen Graham*

Design in Nature

> Look deep into nature, and then you will understand everything better.
>
> —*Albert Einstein*

While doing research for my book I ran into *Design in Nature: How the Constructal Law Governs Evolution in Biology, Physics, Technology, and Social Organization*, a book by Adrian Bejan and J. Peder Zane. Adrian Bejan is J.A. Jones Distinguished Professor of Mechanical Engineering at Duke University. Professor Bejan's research covers a wide range of topics in thermodynamics, heat transfer, fluid mechanics, convection, and porous media. He has received 16 honorary doctorates from universities in 11 countries and is the author of 25 books and 560 peer-referred articles. I had a chance to talk to Professor Bejan on Duke's campus in Durham, North Carolina. (The material that follows is a combination of Professor Bejan's interview with me and another he had with Matt Staggs for Random House's website SUVUDU.com on February 9, 2012.)

Q: Can you explain the constructal law in layman terms?

AB: Everything that moves, whether animate or inanimate, is a flow system. All flow systems generate shape and structures in time in order to facilitate the movement across a landscape filled with resistance. Both a river basin's evolution for moving water from an area (the plain) to a point (the river mouth) and air passages of lungs (a flow system for oxygen) produce tree like structures. Since human beings are part of nature and governed by its laws, the point-to-area or area-to-point flows we construct also tend to be tree-like structures.

Q: How did you discover the constructal law?

AB: I was attending a conference in France where Ilya Prigogine, a Nobel laureate, stated that flow systems—he calls them structures—such as river basins, trees, and lightning are the result of throwing the dice—literally, that's what he said. Around that time I was in the middle of designing cooling systems for computers. The design I ended up with was tree-shaped configurations for sucking heat out of the box. These "trees" on my worktable were based on a principle of deriving heat through the easiest paths of greatest access out of the box. I was making my designs not by copying nature; in fact, that is the complete opposite of what I did: I was inventing trees by invoking a principle.

BIOMIMICRY: LEARNING AND IMITATING NATURE'S DESIGNS

The San Diego Zoo is developing a specialty in biomimicry, a discipline that tries to solve problems by imitating the ingenious and sustainable answers provided by nature. In working session with Procter & Gamble's feminine-care business unit's R&D staff, the zoo's biomimicry experts made an unexpected connection between P&G's problem and the physiology of a gecko. Other ideas came quickly, inspired by flower petals, armadillos, squirrels, and anteaters. By the end of the day, the workgroup had generated eight fresh approaches to the challenges.

—*Dan Heath & Chip Heath, "Made to Stick," Fast Company, November 2009*

BEHOLD THE BIRTH OF VELCRO

The key to visionary achievement is to recognize that everything before you contains the seed of success. When George de Mestral was hiking in a field one day, he noticed little "hitchhikers," small seeds clinging to his trouser legs. Curious, he examined how they had the ability to latch tiny tendrils into the material of his pants. He went back

to his laboratory and tried to replicate the tenacity
of the seed.

—*Alan Cohen*

Similarities between Fruits/Flowers and Creative Ideas: The Natural By-products of the Various Living Systems

There are principles that guide all living systems: humans, trees, and even organizations. For example, nature teaches us that it's not the strongest that survive and thrive but the ones capable of adapting to the ever-changing environment.

The world is emblematic. Parts of speech are
metaphors, because the whole of nature is a meta-
phor of the human mind.

—*Ralph Waldo Emerson*

Nature	Organizations and Humans
If the tree is not sprouting new stems and fruits, it is in the process of dying.	If the enterprise is not creating new value it is in the process of losing market share and fading away.

(continued)

(*continued*)

Nature	Organizations and Humans
Fruits provide the fuel (seeds) for new growth in the forests.	Creative ideas provide fuel for personal and organizational growth.
Flowers add color and enhance the beauty of a bush or tree.	Creative ideas add energy and enhance the company's value.
Saplings grow and become big trees.	Simple ideas unfold and produce big results.
A bush becomes lively through buds and blooming flowers.	A person feels truly alive through creative expression.

Nature always provides an abundance of seeds, larvae, eggs, and so on, to ensure that at least some will survive. In a similar vein, people and organizations need to keep expanding the knowledge and ideas that will ensure their survival as their environment keeps changing.

A corporation is a living organism. It has to continue to shed its skin. Methods have to change. Focus has to change. Values have to change. The sum total of those changes is transformation.

—*Andrew Grove, Intel Founder*

MORE DOTS (EXPANDED KNOWLEDGE BASE)
The First of the Four Requirements (MINT)

Lesson 1: Grow Knowledge
Continually grow your knowledge base, a prerequisite for generating creative ideas.

> Original ideas come from reassembling knowledge in new ways. But you need to have that knowledge in your mind before you can reassemble it.
>
> —*Leon Botstein, President, Bard College*

Lesson 2: Be Persistent
Be persistent in developing your unique talents and nurturing your ideas.

> Talented, motivated, creative people tend to earn more than their peers throughout life.
>
> —*Peter Thiel, Cofounder, PayPal, August 23, 2011,* New York Times

CREATIVITY LESSON 1:
GROW KNOWLEDGE

WHAT'S REVEALED IN NATURE: Fruits are the natural by-products of a healthy and growing tree.

TEACHES US: Creative ideas are like fruits and the natural by-products of a healthy and growing mind.

Creative thinking is connecting dots—your knowledge and life experiences—in imaginative ways. Imagine this: A number of people are faced with the same problem. The creative person among them has more dots, an expanded knowledge base, at his disposal. Because of that, he is able to generate more ideas to solve the problem. The challenge in today's fast-paced lifestyle is to slow down and take time to continually grow your knowledge base (create more dots in our minds). In today's knowledge-driven economy learning capacity determines earning capacity.

> I've told my people that they need to go learn something they haven't done before. I've been a journalist, a lawyer, a CEO. I didn't learn to ski until I was 36. I've learned to scuba dive and fly-fish. It's forced me to be an amateur and to learn to learn. It keeps you humble.
>
> —*Jim Rogers, CEO, Duke Energy*,
> Fortune, *August 17, 2009*

CREATIVITY LESSON 1:
GROW KNOWLEDGE

What's Revealed in Nature?

Fruits are the natural by-products of a healthy and growing tree.

Creativity Lesson

Continually grow your knowledge base is a prerequisite for generating creative ideas.

See this photo in color at www.innovationculture.com.

CREATIVITY LESSON 1:
GROW KNOWLEDGE
Applying the Lesson

The impulse to grow and create is built into us. When we were kids, our natural curiosity helped us learn and grow, and it remains the key to learning and growth throughout our lives and careers.

Stay Curious

While performing surgery to remove cancerous tumors in patients with extremities tumors at Memorial Sloan Kettering Hospital in New York, Dr. Bhaskar Rao often had to perform amputations. But he also learned techniques to save limbs. In 1980 St. Jude Children's Research Hospital in Memphis recruited him. St. Jude Children's Research Hospital is internationally recognized for its pioneering research and treatment of children with cancer and other catastrophic diseases. Ranked one of the best pediatric cancer hospitals in the country, St. Jude is the first and only National Cancer Institute–designated Comprehensive Cancer Center devoted solely to children.

I asked Dr. Rao what gave him the idea to develop these innovative limb-saving techniques.

Dr. Rao said, "I noticed the huge negative impact of amputation on the children's quality of life. Amputation left children with a negative body image. They had significantly less functionality. I wondered, 'What if there was a way to remove the cancerous tumor and also save the limb?' That led to the development of limb-saving surgery." To date he has performed more than 300 limb-saving procedures and initiated programs in Lebanon, Chile, and Brazil.

In the limb-saving procedure, prostheses are implanted to replace the cancerous bone sections that were cut out during the surgery. Because children's bones are still in the growing stage, the prostheses had to be replaced several times to facilitate and keep pace with the normal bone growth process. This required multiple surgeries until the bones stopped growing.

Dr. Rao heard a doctor and scientist in France discuss rephysis, the concept of expandable prosthesis. Using this concept to keep pace with growing bones, the prosthesis could be expanded without surgery using a battery-operated expandable mechanism. The procedure is done without anesthesia, and the patient does not feel any pain. The entire process takes 2 minutes. St. Jude and Dr. Rao invited the doctor to Memphis and worked with him to develop and implement this concept.

Dr. Rao was instrumental in developing the surgical aspect for the International Outreach program at St. Jude, and as director of this program, he travels all over the world and has trained more than 90 pediatric surgeons on the latest and most innovative techniques.

"What has been the key to your growth and success as a sought-after pediatric cancer surgeon?" I asked him.

"My desires to improve children's quality of life and my ever-present curiosity have been the driving factors," was Dr. Rao's reply. He has authored more than 200 academic papers and given more than 400 talks at professional conferences around the world.

> My biggest motivation? Just to keep challenging myself. I see life almost like one long University education that I never had—everyday [*sic*] I'm learning something new.
> —*Richard Branson, Founder & Chairman of Virgin Group*

Every year ask yourself the following question and share the answer with your boss:

Q: How am I more valuable to my organization than I was a year ago?

　A: I'm more valuable because I have more knowledge (more dots) in one or more of the following areas:

- Customers' changing needs (for example, made sales calls to learn firsthand from customers)
- Total business process (spent time in other departments)
- Industry knowledge
- Technological advancements and application
- Competitors' initiatives
- General knowledge

Make a Habit of Asking Questions

The physicist Isadore Rabi, whose scientific work led to the development of radar, the MRI machine, and a Nobel Prize in 1944, was once asked how he became a scientist. Rabi replied that while most of the mothers in the Brooklyn tenement where he grew up asked their children, "What did you learn in school today?" his mother always asked him: "Did you ask any good questions today?"

—*Sheldon H. Gottlieb, MD, FACC, in* Diabetes Forecast, *June 2007*

Seek Assignments beyond Your Job Description

In my career, I always made it a point to ask my bosses if there was something on their plate that I could help them with. My last big promotion at FedEx was the direct result of identifying a need and asking boss to lead a quality action team to improve a business process, unrelated to my responsibilities and job scope at the time.

I've been here 30 years and was promoted, on average, every other year before becoming C.E.O. That's part of what kept me here, because if you're not learning, you're dying. Every time I felt I was at the peak of the learning curve, the company gave me more to do.

In the late 1990s, Leon Gorman, a third-generation member of the family that started L.L. Bean, who was then C.E.O., made me head of the women's

product line. I knew marketing, not products, but
I realized he was developing me to become a
senior leader.

—*Chris McCormick, CEO of L.L. Bean, as told
to Patricia L. Olsen, New York Times,
May 4, 2013*

Don't Confine Your Reading and Learning to Your Field

Our minds can only think to the breadth they are exposed to.
So expose yourself to as many fields as possible.

The creative person wants to be know-it-all. He
wants to know about all kinds of things: ancient
history, nineteenth-century mathematics, current
manufacturing techniques, flower arranging, and
hog futures. Because he never knows when these
ideas might come together to form a new idea. It
may happen six minutes later or six months down
the road. But he has faith that it will happen.

—*Carl Ally, whose agency was responsible for the creative
and memorable ads that helped FedEx become
a household name*

Unless you read different points of view, your mind
will eventually close, and you'll become a prisoner
to a certain point of view that you'll never question.

—*Mohamed El-Erian, CEO, Pimco,
Fortune, July 6, 2009*

Attend Industry Conferences outside Your Field
Expanding your conference attendance beyond your own field allows you to mingle and talk to people in other areas of business. You get exposure to what is happening in their field. How are they applying new technology?

I can recall an idea I suggested and implemented at RCA as a result of my annual visits to the American Management Association's packaging show in New York. The Records division was experiencing pilferage between the warehouse and delivery to the store. The LP records boxes were shipped loose on trucks, making it easy for someone to steal a box. At the show I saw big heat tunnels for shrink-wrapping multiple boxes on a pallet. Implementing this practice at RCA eliminated the theft problem.

> When the economy changes, sometimes, just innovative packaging can put excitement back in a category. For instance, we figured out that the old Snapple bottle wouldn't fit into a car cup holder. So we created a newly designed bottle that the consumer was looking for.
> —*Larry Young, CEO, Dr. Pepper Snapple Group,* Fortune, *May 4, 2009*

Grow Knowledge: Proven Ideas
- Stay curious.
- Every year ask yourself, "How am I more valuable to my organization than I was a year ago?

- Make a habit of asking questions.
- Seek assignments beyond your job description.
- Don't confine your reading and learning to your field.
- Attend industry conferences outside your field.

CREATIVITY LESSON 2: BE PERSISTENT

WHAT'S REVEALED IN NATURE: The growth process from the seed to the fruits takes time and requires steady nurturing.

TEACHES US: Be persistent in developing your unique talents, nurturing your ideas, and pursuing your passion.

Michael Jordan, Steve Jobs, and Tiger Woods were born with natural talents, but it took years of nurturing before their talents reached the levels we admire. Developing natural talents requires ongoing efforts over time. As Voltaire said, "Perfection is attained by slow degrees; she requires the hand of time."

As time passes we gain more knowledge and experience. We get a chance to try out and refine our ideas and techniques. The growth process is not a straight line that is always trending upward. There are plateaus. However, plateaus can be turned into periods of tremendous growth if we use the time and energy for rejuvenation, as well as to polish neglected skills, develop new relationships, reevaluate goals and values, and plan for long-term growth and development.

> Keep searching for that thing you love to do. Once it marries with the thing you're good at, that is priceless.
>
> —*Hugh Jackman*, Parade *magazine, October 9, 2011*

CREATIVITY LESSON 2: BE PERSISTENT
What's Revealed in Nature?

The growth process from the seed to the fruits takes time and requires steady nurturing.

CREATIVITY LESSON

Be persistent in developing your unique talents, nurturing your ideas, and pursuing your passion.

See this photo in color at www.innovationculture.com.

CREATIVITY LESSON 2: BE PERSISTENT
Applying the Lesson

Your unique creative talents are your gift to the world. Nurture and share them. Be patient with yourself as you develop these gifts. There is no shortcut. It requires time and ongoing personal effort.

> I have missed more than 9,000 shots in my career.
> I have lost almost 300 games. On 26 occasions
> I have been entrusted to take the game-winning
> shot . . . and I missed. I have failed over and over
> and over again in my life. And that's precisely why
> I succeed.
>
> —*Michael Jordan, winner of six NBA championships with the Chicago Bulls*

In 2001 an NBA team, the Vancouver Grizzlies, moved to Memphis. In September 2001 Jenny Koltnow joined Memphis Grizzlies Community Investment group as a coordinator. After 14 months Jenny was promoted to manager. In 2004, the Memphis Grizzlies Charitable Foundation was created to expand the team's philanthropy efforts. Jenny was appointed the foundation's executive director.

International Recognition for Grizzlies Philanthropy Work

The Memphis Grizzlies organization was named Sport Team of the Year at the 2012 Beyond Sport Awards for their work in creating positive social change beyond the court. Competing with almost 300 other projects worldwide and professional sports teams spanning six continents, the Grizzlies were highlighted for both the efforts of the Memphis Grizzlies Charitable Foundation and the Memphis Grizzlies Community Investment team, particularly for the Grizzlies TEAM UP Youth Mentoring Initiative.

In a recent meeting I asked Jenny Koltnow to educate me on Grizzlies TEAM UP.

"From the beginning the Grizzlies Foundation has been supporting youth mentoring efforts at agencies throughout the greater Memphis area. In addition to providing financial support we work with the agencies in improving the effectiveness of the mentoring programs. Mentoring typically is one-on-one, that is, one mentor and one student. We noticed that there is a greater need for youth mentoring.

"To meet this need we came up with a model of using a team of three volunteers to mentor a group of nine students. The program design utilizes experiential activities to develop specific skills. The mentoring program is highly structured for developing specific skills. Volunteer mentors are trained on program goals and design.

"TEAM UP began in January 2011 with 15 mentors and 45 students. The goals for the program were:

- "Enhance students' academic achievement and conduct.
- "Help them internalize that high school graduation and college education are personally reachable goals.

- "Help them understand that in today's knowledge-driven economy, postsecondary education is a must for enjoying a successful and financially rewarding career.

"The program results exceeded our expectations. We found that through the team of three mentors the students were exposed to a bigger knowledge and experience base. In 2012 the program was expanded to mentor 162 students."

What is the secret behind the Grizzlies Foundation's and your own success?

"How Can I Run Better" Thinking Carries over to "How Can the Grizzlies Foundation Serve More Youths?"

Jennie Koltnow continues:

"I love running, and it helps me stay in shape. I ran my first marathon in 2004. After the birth of my second son three years ago, I wanted to prove to myself that I could run another marathon. In 2011 I ran the Boston Marathon and raised over $9,000 for the Massachusetts Mentoring Partnership. When I run, I'm thinking, 'Can I run faster than the last time?' As my run time gets better, my self-confidence is also increased.

"This thinking and self-confidence carries over to work. As a team we're always asking, How can the Grizzlies Foundation do better and serve more youths? Every year we reinvent ourselves. I'm constantly looking for best practices in corporate responsibility at other organizations and make it a point to stay in touch with my colleagues around the world. As a result of our recent contact with 'Coaches across America' they'll be sending six coaches to Memphis to assist in youth development at various community centers."

So What If It Takes Five Years to Develop and Pursue Your Unique Talents. Get Started Today!

How many times during the course of a year do you hear someone or even yourself say, "Oh, how I wish I could do that," or "What I'd really like to do is . . . ?" The solution to this kind of thinking came from Professor Crawford in his career counseling class: "If you get started today, you will be there five years from now. Otherwise, you'll still be saying the same thing next year and the year after that."

After getting married, with two kids and a demanding career, I started asking, "Why do we make the life choices we do?" To answer this question I began taking evening classes in the counseling department at the University of Memphis. Before I knew it, I had earned enough credits to earn a master's degree in counseling. My earlier book, *FedEx Delivers*, and this book are the direct results of knowledge gained in the curriculum for that degree.

When I was named head coach of the Chicago Bulls in 1989, my dream was not just to win championships, but to do it in a way that wove together my two greatest passions: basketball and spiritual exploration. On the surface this may sound like a crazy idea, but intuitively I sensed that there was a link between spirit and sport.

—*Phil Jackson, in his book*, Sacred Hoops, *winner of 11 championships as coach and 2 as a player*

Keep Moving Forward

I walk, I run, in the direction of my dreams. Things change along the way, people change, I change, the world changes, even my dreams change. I don't have a place to arrive; I just keep doing what I know how to do the best that I can do it.

—*Shah Rukh Khan, Bollywood superstar at Yale University, April 12, 2012*

Take Full Advantage of Every Learning Opportunity—Every Experience Is a Building Block to a Creative Life

While an undergraduate at Princeton, John Dabiri spent summer at the California Institute of Technology, filming jellyfish at a nearby aquarium and trying to write mathematical models to describe their movement. After graduating with degrees in mechanical and aerospace engineering, he headed to Caltech for good. Dabiri earned his Ph.D. there in 2005 and became a tenured professor before age 30. Along the way, Dabiri, now 32, unraveled some of the mysteries of the jellyfish and how they propel themselves by creating whirling vortexes in the

water. The U.S. Navy is funding development of
underwater craft that employ his mathematical
models to move using 30 percent less energy than
existing options.

—*Olga Kharif*, Businessweek, *April 9, 2012*

Developing Creative Ideas Requires Persistence

Here is a quote that shows how Steve Jobs, after getting fired
from Apple, a company he started, continued to pursue his
creative passions and in the process transformed how ani-
mated movies are made.

Pixar has been a marathon, not a sprint. There are
times when you run a marathon and you wonder,
why am I doing this? But you take a drink of water,
and around the next bend, you get your wind back,
remember the finish line, and keep going.
Fortunately, my training has been in doing things
that take a long time. You know? I was at Apple
10 years; I would have preferred to be there the rest
of my life. So I'm a long-term kind of a person.
I have been trained to think in units of time that are
measured in several years. With what I've chosen to
do with my life, you know, even a small thing takes
a few years. To do anything of magnitude takes at
least five years, more like seven or eight. Rightfully
or wrongfully, that's how I think.

—*Steve Jobs, June 1995, in conversation
with Brent Schlender*, Fast Company,
May 2012

Be Persistent: Proven Ideas

- So what if it takes five years. Get started today!
- Keep moving forward.
- Take full advantage of every learning opportunity— every experience is a building block to a creative life.
- Developing creative ideas requires persistence.

IMAGINATION (TO CONNECT DOTS)
The Second of the Four Requirements (MINT)

Lesson 3: Trust Yourself
Trust that all the resources, including imagination, for germinating creative ideas are within you.

> Executives are constrained not by resources but by their imagination.
>
> —*C.K. Prahalad, Author and Management Thinker*

Lesson 4: Stay Calm
To make and see the imaginative new connections, the mind must be undisturbed.

> People should cultivate curiosity about how exactly things succeed and cultivate "presence of mind" where they deal calmly with problems and let their minds wander freely rather than look for quick answers because they feel stress.
>
> —*Professor Bill Dugan, Columbia Business School, Ideas@Work, December 28, 2012*

CREATIVITY LESSON 3: TRUST YOURSELF

WHAT'S REVEALED IN NATURE: The ingredients for all the fruits are present in the seed.

TEACHES US: The necessary resources for generating creative ideas, including imagination, are within us. They are present in the powerful mind and the even more powerful spirit.

Creativity is connecting dots in imaginative ways. Your brain is a creativity machine. It has a large-capacity hard drive to acquire and store knowledge, which you can also think of as dots that are waiting to be connected. It has boundless imaginative capability. Watch children at play to see imagination in action. Just because you have not exercised your imagination lately does not mean that you have lost this wonderful capability. It needs to be developed and unleashed. Use it or lose it.

> I love that kind of thought. All the information for
> a tree was in an acorn—the tree was somehow
> in there.
> —*Paul McCartney*

However, for the acorn to germinate, it needs the right soil, water, sunlight, and nutrients. We have to create and sustain the right conditions (MINT) for unleashing our natural creative potential.

CREATIVITY LESSON 3: TRUST YOURSELF
What's Revealed in Nature

The ingredients for all the fruits are present in the seed.

CREATIVITY LESSON

Trust that all the resources, including imagination, for germinating creative ideas are within you.

See this photo in color at www.innovationculture.com.

CREATIVITY LESSON 3: TRUST YOURSELF
Applying the Lesson

Following her graduation from Vanderbilt University, Rebecca (Becky) Webb Wilson worked as a Pan Am flight attendant for three years. She got married, changed careers, and became a realtor. After a successful career as a realtor, she decided to go back to school. Upon receiving her law degree, she worked as an assistant United States Attorney for four years. Then Becky became active in her community and played a major role in revitalizing the Memphis Zoo and founding a very effective youth leadership program called Bridge Builders, all while raising four children. She is also a professional nature photographer and has published a book, *Songs of Nature: Meditations in Psalms.*

Q: How did you decide to change careers and enjoy success in such diverse fields?

BW: As a high school exchange student, I spent a summer in the Philippines and really enjoyed it. Working at Pan Am had allowed me to travel around the world. But later, selling real estate did not satisfy my professional needs.

Throughout my years at Vanderbilt I had been very active in the student body government, so I wanted to get back to work in the public sector. Being a trial lawyer and defense attorney interested me. I discussed with

Spence, my husband, about going to law school. I had two children at that time so only took one or two courses at a time. After summer internships and clerking for two circuit court judges, I was offered a position in the U.S. attorney's office. I thoroughly enjoyed my time there. Trying cases, though, was very demanding, both physically and mentally.

Where did I get the courage to make these changes? I guess you could call it delusional or **trust in myself**. I was unencumbered by many self-doubts. The goal, the creative tension between where I was and where I wanted to be, kept me motivated to keep moving forward.

I think my self-confidence came from being the elder daughter and having parents who never told me that I couldn't do anything. My parents let me go to Philippines as an exchange student. In the south at that time it was unheard of to let a 16-year-old girl go alone to live in a foreign country. I was the only American teenager living with a family there and was asked to speak to groups on what life was like in the United States. When I came back to Tennessee, throughout my senior year in high school I spoke to various groups about my experience as an exchange student. These experiences built my confidence not just in public speaking but also in general and taught me to try anything and not limit myself.

Q: Where did you get the idea for Bridge Builders?

BW: Then–Shelby County Mayor Bill Morris took a group of people on a tour of Memphis areas one does not normally see, the bad housing areas, rundown neighborhoods, poverty . . . In my travels with Pan Am I had traveled all over the world, to countries both developed and undeveloped, but did not realize that Memphis had such areas of poverty. It became clear to everyone in the group that we needed to do things differently.

Children were growing up in a segregated environment. I did not want my four children to grow up not being around children who were not as well off as they were. I wanted my children to have a broader view than my experience of growing up in a segregated south.

Every day driving to work in downtown I saw the bridge over the Mississippi river. I thought, What can we do to bridge the gap between people, racially and socioeconomically? What could we do with limited resources to impact young leaders? Put them together so they can get to know each other and learn that they have the same aspirations and are not different.

I was impressed with the Outward Bound program. That physical experience did so much to break down barriers and build self-confidence. So we brought together 20 students, 10 each from an inner-city high school and a private high school, for a one-week Outward Bound–type program. It was a great success. That was 25 years ago, and now Bridge Builders covers all schools in the greater Memphis area and has been expanded to schools in Alabama and Mississippi. Bridge Builders' stated mission: BRIDGES unites and inspires diverse young people to become confident and courageous leaders committed to community transformation.

Q: What did you learn from founding and continuing involvement with Bridge Builders?

BW: What I found is that I am a planner. But instead of starting a meeting by sharing my plans, I learned it is extremely important to hear everybody on the team. The group will come up with a better plan than what one person can. In fact, the leader needs to actively invite other people to share their ideas.

Internalize

We hear and read lots of things that make sense and would be useful in our lives. But as time passes and other demands occupy our attention, these valuable lessons are forgotten. The prerequisite to successful application is internalizing the lesson. The first step for internalizing is reflection. The second step is application to personally experience the benefit of the teaching.

Reflect on the following: Leta Miller in the August 2011 issue of the *Science of Mind* magazine said this:

> Let's consider a tiny basil seed. It is slightly bigger than the period at the end of this sentence. To start its growth process, I cover it with soil that weighs considerably more than the seed itself. It is in the dark. I provide it warmth and moisture. That tiny seed is potent with the life of the Universe! With perfect timing, it breaks open, has the strength to move soil that far outweighs it, and knows which way to grow to reach the light. How does all that happen? It's a glorious mystery to me.
>
> If a tiny seed has that much life force and potential within it, what potency and power are within us? This life force within us is seeking, even demanding, to grow and thrive and be more.

Remind yourself and trust that creativity is in fact the true nature you were born with.

Trust the creative process and focus on creating the four conditions, MINT. Your imagination is a right-brain capability. To unleash that part of your brain, find ways to:

- Actively pursue interests and hobbies.
- Participate in and observe artistic endeavors—music, art, theater.
- Spend time in nature.
- Schedule off-site meetings with speakers who stimulate right-brain thinking.
- Play with children.

Samuel Langhorne Clements held down an adult job as a printer at fourteen, but when his working day ended at three in the afternoon, he headed to the river to swim or fish or navigate a "borrowed" boat. One can imagine that it was there, as he dreamed of becoming a pirate or a trapper or scout, that he became "Mark Twain."

—*Richard Louv*, Last Child in the Woods, *Workman Publishing, New York, 2005*

Spend Time with Children

My son, Naveen, was seven when we moved to Memphis to join FedEx. While playing in the backyard and hearing a plane fly overhead, we looked for the purple and orange colors of the FedEx logo to identify whether it was a FedEx plane. One

Saturday as we were helping my wife plant her summer garden, Naveen says, "Dad, I'm going to plant a small tree and sit on it. As the tree grows taller and taller, I'll go higher and higher in the sky. When the FedEx plane flies over our backyard, I'll look through the pilot's window and say hi to him."

At work that Monday, I had a meeting with the manager of the department responsible for maintaining the plane loaders. My group supplied the spare parts to his mechanics. I observed closely the loader in action—containers were positioned on a platform and the hydraulic lift slowly lifted the containers to the loading door height where they were pulled inside the airplane.

I remember reading *Jack and the Beanstalk* with Naveen as one of his bedtime stories. He connected the dots of storybook knowledge with his desire to reach the plane. I wondered if the engineer who designed the loaders also got the idea from *Jack and the Beanstalk*.

I get my innovation inspiration from children. They have an amazing ability to change ordinary objects into whatever they need them to be by using their imagination. They have the ability to see beyond what is in front of them and create new uses for items. I marvel at how my children can turn a bedroom into a sea, the bed into a pirate ship, pillows into sharks, and empty paper towel rolls into swords.

—*Jamie Woolf, Learning and Development Specialist, Kimberly-Clark*

Stretch Your Thinking: Right-Brain Thinking Development at IBM

People need experiences at "getting out of the box" if they are to do so when it matters. One interesting approach is practiced by CEO Lou Gerstner at IBM. Every six weeks he takes his top 40 managers off-site for a two-day retreat. But these are not typical operating reviews. Rather, they are dedicated to management learning in nontraditional areas. Each session features an outside speaker who addresses a topic that is peripheral to the immediate concerns of IBM's leadership. These speakers may be academics, executives from other industries, or even representatives of the art world. Gerstner personally leads these sessions; his objective is to give his executives practice in stretching their thinking and developing new perspectives on IBM's business.

—*Michael Hammer and Steven A. Stanton, "The Power of Reflection,"* Fortune, *November 24, 1997*

Trust Yourself: Proven Ideas

- Internalize that you have all the resources within to generate creative ideas.

- Remind yourself and trust that creativity is, in fact, the true nature you were born with.

- To reignite your imagination, spend time with children.

- Stretch your thinking by listening and talking about areas beyond your profession.

CREATIVITY LESSON 4: STAY CALM

WHAT'S REVEALED IN NATURE: To see a clear reflection in a lake or pond, the water must be clear and undisturbed.

TEACHES US: To make and see the imaginative new connections, the mind must be undisturbed.

When we are in a state of peace and serenity, we see things more clearly, we think more lucidly, and we speak and act with greater conviction. We can step back and look at the big picture. But an agitated mind is not capable of thinking clearly and formulating the big picture. The neurons in an agitated mind take the path of least resistance—the way things have always been done—instead of exploring new pathways to generate creative options.

> When you are inspired by some great purpose,
> some extraordinary project, all your thoughts break
> their bounds: Your mind transcends limitations,
> your consciousness expands in every direction, and
> you find yourself in a new, great, and wonderful
> world. Dormant forces, faculties, and talents come
> alive, and you discover yourself to be a greater
> person by far than you ever dreamed yourself to be.
> —*Patanjali, Indian Scholar, First-Century BC*

> The creative process is a process of surrender, not
> control.
> —*Julia Cameron,* The Artist's Way, *New York: Penguin
> Putnam, 1992*

CREATIVITY LESSON 4: STAY CALM
What's Revealed in Nature

To see a clear reflection in a lake or pond, the water must be clear and undisturbed.

CREATIVITY LESSON

To make and see imaginative new connections, the mind must be undisturbed.

See this photo in color at www.innovationculture.com.

CREATIVITY LESSON 4: STAY CALM
Applying the Lesson

Gayle Rose is founder and CEO of Electronic Vault Services (EVS), a data backup and storage solutions company. In addition to being a successful entrepreneur and business executive, she is a very active community leader. She played a lead role in landing the Grizzlies NBA basketball team in Memphis.

In 1995 under Mertie Buckman's leadership, a group of women, including Gayle, gathered to explore an idea: If women pooled their resources, they could accomplish more in their community than each could individually. Right after that meeting, Gayle saw a story in the local newspaper about Oseola McCarty. Miss McCarty, an African American cleaning woman from Mississippi, donated $250,000 to the University of Southern Mississippi for a student scholarship program. At the time this was by far the largest gift ever given to the University of Southern Mississippi by an African American.

The remarkable thing was that Miss McCarty had accumulated this large amount from doing laundry at $1.50 to $2 a bundle. Gayle realized, "Miss McCarty would be the ideal person to inspire the group in Memphis to join the women in philanthropy initiative." She called Miss McCarty to invite her to speak to the Memphis group. Miss McCarty's response was that she did not want to travel. Gayle asked, "Can I come to your place to shoot a video?"

Gayle took a crew to Mississippi and shot an 8-minute video. The video eventually was seen by President Bill Clinton, who then invited Miss McCarty and Gayle to a special White House ceremony to award the Presidential Citizens Medal, the nation's second highest civilian award, to Miss McCarty. The huge publicity of this story in Memphis produced the result Gayle was looking for—an inspired group of women representing a broad cross section came together and launched the Women's Foundation for a Greater Memphis.

I asked Gayle, "What's the secret to your success, both on and off the job?"

Meditation in the Morning Keeps Mind Calm All Day

"Customers store their critical data with us and want to be able to recover fully without any negative impact to their operations and systems in case of a problem. It's a very demanding and time-sensitive business. I start my day with 30 minutes of meditation. This 30-minute investment helps me greatly in staying calm throughout the day. I exercise in the evening. The exercise helps in not just staying healthy but also in releasing the stress built up during the day.

"EVS is a pioneer in cloud storage, and we have to keep innovating to stay ahead of the competition and meet the changing needs of our customers. Technology is changing fast. I have a network of individuals in the technology field who I talk to regularly. They help my team, and I stay current with the latest advancements in technology."

A Balanced Lifestyle Leads to a Balanced Mind

A balanced mind is a calm mind, a natural by-product of a balanced lifestyle celebrating life in its fullness. Unmet life needs do not go away—they create inner conflicts. Give yourself permission to take time for recharging your batteries.

> I believe much more strongly now than ever that to be able to be good at what I do, I need to be good to myself, creatively, and refill my own creative well before I can be any less than a brain-dead zombie.
> —*Mary Kole*, *Literary Agent*, *CNN.com*,
> *May 24, 2011*

Take Time to Enjoy Life's Simple Pleasures

> Don't take every day for granted; savor the hot bath, the scent of wood-smoke, the comfort of blankets, the sweet smell of newly baked bread, the wonders of early morning birdsong. To access our creative powers, we need only be in awe of the mystery of the universe, and open to its presence in our lives in both the large and small moments.
> —*Dan Wakefield*, Creating from the Spirit,
> *New York: Ballatine, 1996*

Commune with Nature and Experience Peace

We are part of nature at large. When we commune with nature's beauty and serenity, we connect with our beautiful and serene self—the imaginative and creative self.

In a *Newsweek* story by Paul Theroux, Martin Scorsese commented on his friend George Harrison. He was quoted as saying:

> Whatever problems he had, he was still out there, doing gardening himself. Maybe it's meditation. It helped to cut away the madness of the world around him. It fascinates me to think that he creates music like this and he gardens! And, he does everything in between. It gives him a different way of looking at life. The reality of it is that it's a way of finding some peace with yourself.

> Your body and brain demand rest to produce the chemicals you need to think new thoughts. Otherwise, all you are doing is rearranging and recycling the same old thoughts.
> —*Peter Oswald, MD*

Gather Detailed Information and Take a Calm Look at the Big Picture

Every department in FedEx operates as a critical component of a highly integrated system. In this hub-and-spoke operating system, one late-arriving flight from any place in the world affects the entire system.

My team found the following process very effective in finding creative solutions to FedEx's service problems during the double-digit growth years:

1. Gather detailed information about current systems, processes, and operations.

2. Put the gathered information/flow charts on the wall to formulate the big picture.

3. Stare at the big picture and ask, "Why are we doing it this way?" and "What if we make this change in this process?"

4. The creative connections/solutions will jump out at you from the wall.

The key to success in this process is a calm and imaginative mind.

Stay Calm: Proven Ideas

- Meditation in the morning keeps mind calm all day.
- A balanced lifestyle leads to a balanced and calm mind.
- Take time to enjoy life's simple pleasures.
- Commune with nature and experience peace.
- For creative problem solving, gather detailed information about the problem and take a calm look at the big picture.

Nominal Stress (Creative Tension)
The Third of the Four Requirements (MINT)

Lesson 5: Take Risks
Take the risk inherent in setting innovation goals (creative tension) and expressing your imperfect ideas.

> Whatever you strive for, don't dwell on construct-
> ing the perfect plan or search for the flawless
> solution, because perfect can be the enemy of
> progress. Have the confidence to forge ahead with a
> good enough plan, with imperfect knowledge.
> Then continually adjust, adapt, and learn.
> —*Greg Brown, Chairman, Motorola Solutions,
> Rutgers commencement*, Bloomberg Businessweek,
> *May 28, 2012*

Lesson 6: Minimize Negativity
Minimize internal and external negative influences that obstruct creative energy flow.

> Our ultimate freedom is the right and power to
> decide how anybody or anything outside ourselves
> will affect us.
> —*Stephen Covey*

CREATIVITY LESSON 5: TAKE RISKS

WHAT'S REVEALED IN NATURE: Trees do not have to be perfect to be beautiful and productive.

TEACHES US: Take the risk inherent in setting innovation goals (creative tension) and expressing your imperfect ideas.

Setting Innovation Goals (Creative Tension)

The creative process involves taking risks and overcoming stress. If the boss has not set up an innovation goal, identify an area of improvement that you or your team have a direct impact on, take the initiative, and set an improvement goal. Yes, it's full of risk and creates stress because early on you probably don't know how your team will achieve it. But it is this innovation initiative, the needed creative tension, that will separate you and your team from others in the organization.

Expressing Raw Creative Ideas

All creative ideas are raw at first. They're not fully developed, because not every detail has been worked out. The thought of sounding stupid holds you back. But you have to take the risk inherent in expressing raw creative ideas. This allows others to work with you on developing the details.

CREATIVITY LESSON 5: TAKE RISKS
What's Revealed in Nature

Trees do not have to be perfect to be beautiful and productive.

CREATIVITY LESSON

Take the risks inherent in setting innovation goals (creative tension) and expressing your imperfect ideas.

See this photo in color at www.innovationculture.com.

CREATIVITY LESSON 5: TAKE RISKS
Applying the Lesson

Jay Myers, entrepreneur and author, started Interactive Solution Inc. (ISI) in 1996 with one engineer and a part-time secretary to provide customized, integrated solutions in video conferencing and audiovisual technologies. ISI integrates the latest components and software into customized systems that connect organizations to their workers and to the world. ISI has provided customized solutions for corporate communications, interagency communications, distance learning, telemedicine, and more.

In a recent four-year period (2007–2011), including the Great Recession, ISI's annual revenue grew from $11 million to $25 million. I asked Jay, "What was the reason behind this tremendous growth?"

Take the Risk and Ask Customers, "What Would You Like?"

> "We don't go in with solutions. We ask the customers, 'What would you like to see?' While working with a hospital to develop a tele-medicine solution we asked the nurse, the end user, what she would like to see. She requested that the cart housing the system be easy to move and use. We designed a light cart that a nurse can move easily

without much force and incorporated features that made the system easy to use.

"The customer response to our questions provides the needed creative tension for our sales and engineering people to apply their creativity toward innovative business solutions. During these conversations customers often share with us their design ideas as to how they would design the system. You should see the expression of pride on their face when they see the delivered product reflecting their design suggestions.

"Our first telemedicine system was developed to connect North Mississippi Medical in Tupelo with Le Bonheur Children's Hospital in Memphis. Tupelo needed access to Le Bonheur's pediatric cardiology specialists to care for their patients. Seeing the success of this installation we asked, 'What if other medical specialties also had customized tele-medicine solutions?' Since then we've added medical specialties such as dermatology; ear, nose, and throat (ENT); and others in our ISI-MD systems. We're the country's largest tele-medicine systems provider with over 3,000 installed systems.

"For our distance learning systems we asked the educators, 'What's holding you back?' Their responses led us to designing a user friendly system, ISI-Educator, with touch screen panels."

Ask, "How Do We Differentiate Ourselves?"

Jay Myers of ISI continues:

> "We regularly ask ourselves how do we differentiate ourselves from the competition? As a result of this internal conversation we came up with a product called ISI-NET. With this product we can remotely access all our carts. We can run diagnostics remotely. The system alerts us in advance of any potential problems, allowing us to do preventive maintenance and eliminate downtime. Customers love it. We and the customer can produce all the reports. This has differentiated us from other vendors."

Believe Every Process, Product, or Service Can Be Better and Challenge Yourself to Make It Better

If you believe every system can be made better, it becomes natural to set improvement and innovation goals. This creates the required tension in the mind for it to go to work generating what ifs. This is the underlying philosophy of the industrial engineering discipline, the subject of my graduate studies at the Illinois Institute of Technology. Every area in the business world is a candidate for improving productivity or enhancing customer experience through the application of technology.

Watch Self-Censoring

Don't censor your idea just because you think it's not perfect and the details haven't all been worked out. If you're not

100 percent sure, then you can preface your idea by saying, "I haven't worked out all the details but what if . . . ?"

You don't know where the collective imagination of people on the team might take this imperfect idea. Don't censor yourself just because the boss is in the room and you don't want to sound stupid. In fact, all of my promotions at RCA and FedEx were the direct results of taking risks and sharing ideas when my bosses were in the room. Your ideas are valuable and necessary.

> A bird doesn't sing because it has an answer; it sings because it has a song.
>
> —*Lou Holtz, Football Coach and Motivational Speaker*

Learn to Successfully Deal with Stress

> Creativity is unpredictable and disruptive. The quest for a new idea often inspires fear—about whether the idea is the right one; whether executing it is possible; whether the costs of change will swamp its benefits.
>
> —*Robert Safian, Editor,* Fast Company *magazine, June 2011*

As the preceding quote shows, fear and stress are part of work life. It is also true that an overly stressed mind is not in a creative mode. A stressed mind is in a survival mode. I successfully handle stress with a personal philosophy: "If there is a problem, there is a solution. In fact, there are multiple solutions to every problem. Our job is to focus on finding the best solution." This operating philosophy reduces stress and provides the needed creative space for exploring what ifs.

Learn to Live with Lack of Swift Resolution

The mind does not like stress, and it wants stress resolved as soon as possible. Those of us who are analytically inclined and pride ourselves on being quick problem solvers feel stressed when problems stay unresolved. Creative problem solving sometimes requires living temporarily with ambiguity to give mind the time and space to play the connecting dots game.

Allow Others to Help You

All creative ideas at first are raw, not fully developed or thought out. But they still have great potential to make a big difference. Also, anything truly creative results in change.

And if there is one thing that is hard to reconcile with comfort zones, routines, policies, and not-invented-here attitude, it's change. Yes, it's risky expressing raw, creative ideas. We withhold our talents in fear of failure or of what others might think if we put ourselves out there. We withhold our ideas to avoid rocking the boat. But I have experienced firsthand that once shared, the idea becomes a basis for others to build upon. Risk is worth taking, and it's the key to career success.

After we leave school, we tend to head down one of two roads: (1) We close our minds to new or different information while becoming more and more sure of ourselves; or (2) we watch, listen, and learn as we get older. The second road has way more bumps and curves, but it's also the path to wisdom.

—*Marilyn vos Savant*, Parade *magazine, November 13, 2011*

Take Risk: Proven Ideas

- Take the risk and ask customers, "What would you like?"
- Ask, "How do we differentiate ourselves?"
- Believe every process, product, or service can be better because it can be.
- Watch self-censoring.
- Learn to successfully deal with stress.
- Learn to live with lack of swift resolution of problems.
- Allow others to help you.

CREATIVITY LESSON 6:
MINIMIZE NEGATIVITY

WHAT'S REVEALED IN NATURE: There are elements in the environment like storms, bugs, and diseases that can damage trees or destroy fruits.

TEACHES US: Minimize internal and external negative influences that obstruct your creative energy flow.

An environment of excessively critical people, inner insecurity, fear of failure, and stress diminish a person's capacity for generating creative ideas. We're a product of our external influences. Pessimistic people can be a negative influence and a drain on our creative energy. Fear narrows the paths in the brain for neurons to travel and make new connections.

We cannot completely eliminate these distractions, but we can take actions to minimize them. The first step is to identify the factors and how they are blocking your creativity. Then take the appropriate preventive measures to minimize them and their negative influence.

> Do not allow people to dim your shine because they are blinded. Tell them to put on some sunglasses.
>
> —*Lady Gaga, Quotes*, Reader's Digest, *March 2012*

CREATIVITY LESSON 6:
MINIMIZE NEGATIVITY
What's Revealed in Nature

There are elements in the environment like storms, bugs, and diseases that can damage trees or destroy fruits.

CREATIVITY LESSON

Minimize internal and external negative influences that obstruct your creative energy flow.

See this photo in color at www.innovationculture.com.

Creativity Lesson 6:
Minimize Negativity

Applying the Lesson

I had read about Don Hutson in the local media and occasionally had seen him in the national media. After completing his undergraduate work at the University of Memphis with a sales major, he joined a seminar company, promoting and selling tickets for its seminars. Now he is chairman and CEO of U.S. Learning, LLC, a Memphis-based sales training firm, as well as a *New York Times* bestselling coauthor of *The One Minute Entrepreneur* and a globally recognized speaker who has given approximately 6,000 talks in 34 countries.

I wanted to know the story behind Don's very creative and successful career journey, so I sent him an e-mail requesting a meeting. To my pleasant surprise I received a reply within a few hours advising me that he was in Las Vegas recording an Interactive Virtual Sales Training program but would be happy to meet the following week when he was back in Memphis.

After explaining to him my book concept, I asked Don to walk me through his career journey that got him to where he is today. During this 1-hour conversation I noticed his application of many of the *Unleashing Creativity* lessons. Following are some of the key steps Don took to reach the lofty goals he set for himself. (The following material is a combination of Don's interview with me and another he had with John Branston of *Memphis Business Quarterly*, published in its Winter 2010 issue.)

Grow Knowledge: "I'm an avid reader. For a specific area of interest, I research what books I need to read. I get all the books on the subject I can find and I read them. One of my first purchases was a book by Orison Marden that I bought for 25 cents at a garage sale. I had no clue as to who Marden was. But I liked the book title, *The Miracle of Right Thought*. I read it cover to cover and found it very powerful. Then I found out he wrote 46 books. I have 42 of them. My home on South Bluff along the Mississippi River is built around my favorite room in the house, a library that houses 8,000 books. I probably have one of the largest collections of self-help books."

Be Persistent: "Ken Blanchard, author of the mega-seller *The One Minute Manager*, and I were in a Speakers Roundtable for many years with a mentor named Charlie Tremendous Jones. I proposed to Ken that we coauthor a book titled *The One Minute Mentor* as a tribute to Tremendous. He found the concept interesting but not enough to get involved immediately due to his busy schedule. Our young coauthor, Ethan Willis, suggested we change the focus to entrepreneurship. Ken liked that idea, and the three of us collaborated on the book. The result was *The One Minute Entrepreneur*, a number one

New York Times best seller. The whole process from start to finish took five years."

Trust Yourself: "After working for the sales training company out of college, I had saved up some money and decided then that I wanted to start my own business. But I had a wife and a child. My dad said, 'Don, do you know what you're doing?' I had received lots of positive feedback on my sales presentations, and I said, 'Dad, I'm confident that I can do it.' Once he realized my confidence, he encouraged me to follow my passion. I also believe that luck plays a part in your success, and I got some good breaks along the way."

Minimize Negativity
Practices Used by Don to Deal with Internal and External Negativity

Negative Influences: "After graduating from the University of Memphis, I went to work for a sales training firm. We had to give speeches to small groups. At age 21 I was scared to death and felt incompetent, but I had a good manager and over time I got pretty good. My first 1,500 speeches were little 30-minute freebies to six or eight people. That's where I paid my dues. My first paid speech was in Atlanta for Southeastern LP Gas Association. I think I was paid $150."

Don't Make It Personal: "I've lost sales I thought I'd make. Being in sales you have to constantly deal with rejection. I don't take it personally. I analyze what I need to do to recalibrate and get back to making more calls. To deal with negativity/ rejection/setbacks, you need to be strong emotionally. Otherwise you're operating from a weak foundation."

Go toward Prosperity Instead of Scarcity: "In times of challenge we can go toward abundance and prosperity or we can go toward scarcity. Too many people go toward scarcity, and they freak out too early and they give up too soon. I operate with a philosophy that there are no unrealistic goals, only unrealistic timeframes."

Develop and Build on Your Strengths: "After the success of *The One Minute Entrepreneur* book, I collaborated with Dr. George Lucas and coauthored *The One Minute Negotiator*. I enjoy reading, writing, and sharing. I've authored or coauthored 13 books and many videos. My strength is teaching people 'How to sell value rather than price' and 'Focus on possibilities rather than problems.'"

Use the Power of Positive Speaking

We've all heard and read about the power of positive thinking. I've found that the best way to create a positive and receptive atmosphere for creative ideas is to utilize the power of positive speaking. Take a look at two possible versions of a common scenario:

Someone presents a creative idea.

Option A: You respond, "It won't work."

- The presenter asks, "Why?"
- You share your concern as to why you think it won't work.
- The presenter answers with a possible solution to overcome the obstacle stated by you.

But your mind, instead of listening to his answer, is thinking of the next obstacle you're going to bring up to prove that the idea won't work. Because when your mind heard the message that it won't work, its mission became to *prove* that it won't work.

After addressing the unending list of problems brought up by you, the presenter gets frustrated and gives up. Because of the feeling that he wasn't listened to, the presenter vows to not voice his ideas in the future.

Option B: You respond, "That's a great idea. There are a couple of things I'm not clear on . . . please help me understand."

- You share your concern as to why you think it won't work.
- The presenter answers with a possible solution to overcome the obstacle stated by you.

This time your mind is listening to understand his answer instead of thinking of the next obstacle you're going to bring up to prove that the idea won't work, because your mind got the message that it's a great idea and wants to understand. Now, two minds are engaged in finding solutions to your genuine concerns.

Even though all of your concerns were not successfully addressed in the meeting, the presenter leaves the meeting feeling good. "I'll work on the unresolved issues and get back to you in few weeks." He feels that he was listened to. Your example will motivate others in giving ideas a positive reception.

> Whatever anybody says or does, assume positive intent . . . When you assume negative intent, you're angry.
> —*Indra Nooyi, Chairman and CEO, PEPSICO,*
> Fortune, *May 12, 2008*

Surround Yourself with People Who Make You Better

During his 2012 commencement address at MIT, Salman Khan, founder of Khan Academy, said, "There will be pessimism and cynicism everywhere. It is easy to succumb to this, to become cynical or negative yourself. If you do, you with the potential that you have, it would be a loss for yourself and for humanity. To fight these forces of negativity, to increase the net positivity in the world, to optimize the happiness of yourself and the people you love, here are some tips and tools that I like to return to. I am not too much older than most of you, so take all of this with a large grain of salt.

"Start every morning with a smile—even a forced one—it will make you happier. Replace the words 'I have to' with 'I get to' in your vocabulary. Smile with your mouth, your eyes, your ears, your face, your body at every living thing you see. Be a source of energy and optimism. **Surround yourself with people who make you better**. Realize or even rationalize that the grass is truly greener on your side of the fence. Just the belief that it is becomes a self-fulfilling prophecy."

Be on Guard against Your Ego Making Everything Personal

There is the healthy ego, the one that allows you to have self-confidence, the confidence based on your past efforts and success in solving problems. This confidence makes you look at problems as opportunities to grow, rather than obstacles to fear. There is also the unhealthy ego, the one that makes you think that only you have the right answer and your way of solving problems is the only way. Unhealthy ego makes everything about "me and my." When people voice concerns about your idea, the unhealthy ego makes it personal. It influences you to respond in a manner that is not conducive to engaging others in creative problem solving. Bear in mind that people's comments are about the idea and not about you as a human being.

Make a decision to relinquish the need to control, the need to be approved, and the need to judge.

Those are the three things the ego is doing
all the time.

—*Deepak Chopra, Best-Selling Author*

Keep the Switch in the On Position

Feeling positive about yourself and others keeps the creativity switch in the on position. In this state you're open to ideas from within and from others. Negativity kills imagination. It stifles learning and growth. Negativity is the off switch.

Some of the most amazing things have been
accomplished by people others thought were crazy.
So let your actions flow freely without negativity,
apprehension, or self-consciousness.

—*Allison Arden, Author*, Book of Doing, *New York: Penguin Group, 2012*

Be Aware of Self-Imposed Limits

Once upon a time, we believed that the world was
flat—that beyond a certain point, there would be
nowhere to go. And though we now know the
world is round, we still fear falling off imaginary
edges, too often thinking there's only so far we can
stretch, so hard we can push. The most dangerous
limits are those in our own head. When you feel
you're at your edge, look again. You can go farther.

—SELF *magazine, February 2012*

So What If You Made a Mistake? It's Not the End of the World

> I entered my first violin competition . . . I began playing and I messed it up worse than I ever could have imagined . . . I turned to the audience and said, "I'd like to start over." I got into this zone of feeling completely liberated and relaxed because I knew I had lost. I played the best I had ever played in my life . . . For me it was a major revelation, and it taught me that when you take your mind off worrying about being perfect all the time, sometimes amazing things can happen.

> —*Joshua Bell, Grammy Award for best performance with orchestra*, Newsweek, *January 9, 2012*

Minimize Negativity: Proven Ideas

- Be on guard against your ego making everything personal.
- Go toward prosperity instead of scarcity.
- Develop and build on your strengths.
- Use the power of positive speaking.
- Surround yourself with people who make you better.
- Feeling positive about yourself keeps the creativity switch in the on position.
- Be aware of self-imposed limits.
- So what if you made a mistake? It's not the end of the world.

TIME (TO THINK AND NURTURE IDEAS)
The Fourth of the Four Requirements (MINT)

Lesson 7: Unplug Your Devices
Schedule quiet time for creative thinking by turning off all electronic devices.

> Don't check your e-mail when you're creating. Nothing earth-shattering is going to happen in an hour or two.
>
> —*Anna Rabinowitz*, O *magazine, February 2011*

> The priority is creating time for silence so we can process ideas, react instinctively to them, give them strong business foundations, and ensure they are in line with the idea that launched us in the first place.
>
> —*Natalie Massenet, Founder and Executive Chairman of the Net-A-Porter Group*, Bloomberg Businessweek, *April 15–April 21, 2013*

CREATIVITY LESSON 7:
UNPLUG YOUR DEVICES

WHAT'S REVEALED IN NATURE: Trees grow and produce fruits in silence.

TEACHES US: Schedule quiet time for creative thinking by turning off all electronic devices.

Almost all innovations, whether technical, political, or social, come from thinking deeply about the subject. That means taking time to learn, think, and imagine. My most favorite mini-vacations are long weekends on a lake or in the mountains. Recently, we rented a cabin on Lake Ouachita in Arkansas, a beautiful hideaway with woods surrounding the lake. In addition to being very relaxing, the hours spent on the cabin deck with the smartphone turned off were very productive in generating ideas for this book.

Empathy, as well as deep thought, depends (as neuroscientists like Antonio Damasio have found) on neural processes that are "inherently slow." The very ones our high-speed lives have little time for.

—*Pico Iyer*, *"The Joy of Quiet,"* New York Times, *December 29, 2011*

Creativity Lesson 7:
Unplug Your Devices
What's Revealed in Nature

Trees grow and produce fruits in silence.

Creativity Lesson

Schedule quiet time for creative thinking by turning off all electronic devices.

See this photo in color at www.innovationculture.com.

CREATIVITY LESSON 7:
UNPLUG YOUR DEVICES
Applying the Lesson

Carol Roberts began her career with International Paper as associate engineer at the Mobile, Alabama, mill. In 1991 she became mill manager at the Oswego, New York, facility. In 1993, Carol was promoted to general manager of kraft packaging. From there she moved to the corporate office as vice president of people development. In 2005 she was named senior vice president of industrial packaging. In 2011 she was named chief financial officer (CFO). International Paper is a highly successful global company with annual revenue that exceeded $27 billion in 2011.

> I asked Carol, "What's the secret behind your success in such diverse functions as engineering, manufacturing, human resource development, and finance?"
>
> Carol replied: "If you're looking for a common thread it would be,
> 1. "My need to make a difference—I'm constantly looking for what's going to make a difference.
> 2. "Do my best in whatever I'm working on.
> 3. "And, I love to do things with a team of people.
>
> "Through creative problem solving I was able to make a difference in each position and help take the department to the next level. As vice president of people development I first identified management and leadership skills required to take

International Paper to the next level. Then I put in place a Performance Development Roadmap to help develop these skills. As senior vice president of industrial packaging, I led the acquisition of Weyerhaeuser Company's containerboard, packaging, and recycling business."

I then asked, "Creative problem solving requires time to collect the information (dots) and time to connect these dots creatively. With all the day-to-day responsibilities and demands on your time, how do you find time to think?"

Making Time to Think Part of Your Daily Routine

Carol answered, "Yes, finding time to think is the biggest challenge. Most days I run before I get to work. On weekends my runs are even longer. When I'm running, I'm completely in the moment and relaxed. The mind is free connecting dots, and I often finish with ideas after these runs.

"After arriving at the office, I like to read the *New York Times* and the *Wall Street Journal*. This allows me to step back and look at the bigger picture, what's happening in the world at large.

"My natural style is to engage my mind with my staff. Being an engineer by education and training, I'm constantly looking for information, more dots. The CFO role is new to me. I don't know much about taxes and insurance. I gather the group and ask them to educate me. I ask lots of 'why?' People love to talk about their areas. They give me information, and I engage them in connecting dots in imaginative ways.

"I'm big on alignment, making sure everybody on the team is aligned on the strategic direction. I give them the context, the why behind the strategic goals. I focus on creating the safe environment for everyone and getting out of the way. I've learned to not get into the day-to-day details. This gives them and me the needed time and space to engage the mind in creative thinking."

Schedule "Think Time" on Your Calendar

The proven way for developing creative solutions to business problems is to generate lots of ideas. This requires time to think without the distraction of flashing or beeping devices. If we are busy attending meetings all day and engaged with technology 24/7, where is the time to focus and think? For creative problem solving, your calendar must reflect a balance between doing and thinking.

A story in the May 21, 2012, issue of *Fortune* reported that every few months, David Cote, CEO of Honeywell International, set aside a day to sit alone in his office reflecting on big ideas. He turned up the iTunes and did not take phone calls. It was during these solitary sessions that he decided to concentrate on the three grand themes of energy efficiency, energy conservation, and safety.

> Think left and think right and think low and think
> high. Oh, the things you can think up if only
> you try.
>
> —*Theodor Geisel (Dr. Seuss)*

Become an In-House Management Consultant

Make a practice of taking time to use the two most powerful tools in innovation: why and what if. When you question accepted assumptions behind the current business processes or the business models, you discover opportunities. Some-time to avoid hurting egos you may have to be diplomatic in asking questions. Preface your question with, "Help me understand why we are . . . ?" This is what an outside consultant does and in that process is able to see opportunities for improvement. Become an in-house consultant and build a reputation as the person others in the organization turn to for creative business solutions.

> Leading a closely watched, high-growth company
> can be frenetic. One of the biggest problems:
> finding the time to be pro-active rather than reac-
> tive. But Bezos (Amazon CEO), at the end of each
> quarter, solves this by just going away. His solo
> retreats have been put to good effect, resulting in
> several new ideas and products, including Amazon's
> fulfillment center for third-party sellers.
> —*Fortune, April 9, 2012*

Schedule Think Time at the Workgroup Level

Twice a year, Ken, my boss at FedEx, planned an off-site planning session with those who reported directly to him. The purpose of the session was to review the group's performance against the goals and objectives for the current fiscal year and to brainstorm ideas to bridge the gap. Being away from the telephones and other distractions allowed the workgroup to focus on the area under review and discussion. We always came back with creative ideas that helped FedEx not just to achieve but also to exceed its growth revenue and profit targets for the year.

> Last week, Adweek named Oliver Francois, Chief Marketing Officer for Fiat and Chrysler, its Grand Brand Genius for 2012. Advertising Age, a competing publication, named him Marketer of the Year . . . Francois likes to hold brainstorming sessions in his office for new advertising campaigns. The meetings can last hours. "It is a very intimate conversation, typically. The creative reviews are fewer people versus more people," said Marissa Hunter, director of marketing for the Ram brand. "It tends to be very collaborative process."
> —*Chicago Tribune, December 16, 2012*

Give Yourself Permission to Unplug

Just when I started to work on my book *FedEx Delivers*, I switched to playing golf, having previously played tennis for many years. I loved being outdoors in nature on the golf course with friends.

I have a TV in my home office. I found myself turning on the golf channel to watch the professionals playing on the PGA tour every hour or so throughout the day. These frequent interruptions significantly slowed down the progress on the manuscript. After every break it took time for my mind to get back to the creative place where it was before the interruption. I called DISH TV to switch to a package that did not include the Golf Channel. Yes, it seemed a drastic action, but I found there was more than enough golf on the other channels to watch over the weekends when I was not working on the book.

> The toughest part was disconnecting from all my devices, especially as I was running an online media company. I thought people would need an answer, things would be left undone. I had to get better at living with incompletion . . . It wasn't easy. It is a process . . . I start my day by meditating. I do yoga. I've tried to stop multitasking. I am much more able to deal with challenges. I think I'm more creative because I don't miss the subtle things, what Steve Jobs called listening to the whisperings.
>
> —*Arianna Huffington as told to Diane Brady*, Bloomberg Businessweek, *March 18–March 24, 2013*

Use Lunch Time to Get Away from the Desk

> At lunch I will go out and bike 20 miles. Then I'll get back and all of a sudden a thought comes to my brain, and I solve something I was struggling with. Goodnight (CEO of SAS) understands the innovative process, and there's time built for it.
>
> —*Mary Simmons, Principal Software Developer, SAS*, Fortune, *August 17, 2009*

Unplug Your Devices: Proven Ideas

- Give yourself permission to unplug.
- Make time to think part of your daily routine.
- Schedule think time on your personal calendar.
- Become an in-house management consultant.
- Schedule think time at the workgroup level.
- Use lunch time to get away from the desk.

Edison's friends in Florida respected his need for privacy. He would go out to the end of his dock and sit and fish—but he'd fish without any bait on his line. Edison was not interested in catching fish; he was after time to think.

—*James Newton*, Uncommon Friends,
Harcourt Brace, 1987

PART IV

The Tested and Proven Three-Step Innovation Process

Innovation is the generation, acceptance,
and implementation of new ideas,
processes, products, or services. It can
thus occur in any part of a corporation, and
it can involve creative use as well as
original invention. Application and
implementation are central to this
definition; it involves the capacity
to change or adapt.

—Rosabeth Moss Kanter, in her
landmark book, *The Change Masters*

I came to see, in my time at IBM, that
culture isn't just one aspect of the game—it
is the game. In the end, an organization is

> nothing more than the collective capacity
> of its people to create value.
>
> —Lou Gerstner, CEO, IBM in his book, *Who Says
> Elephants Can't Dance?*

INNOVATION: A THREE-STEP PEOPLE PROCESS

Whereas creativity deals solely with the generation of ideas by exploring what if scenarios, innovation starts with creative ideas but takes the process two steps further.

Innovation does not just happen. It must be actively supported. Individual employee creativity is the first step of innovation. Managers/team leaders have to create an environment where employees feel comfortable in suggesting and experimenting with new ways of doing things.

An innovation culture actively promotes the three stages of innovation:

- Generation
- Acceptance
- Implementation

It's people who have creative ideas. It's people who accept and develop the raw creative ideas. It's people who successfully implement the developed ideas. Leaders at all levels of the organization play the single most important role in creating and sustaining the supportive environment that actively engages people in the innovation process, developing and unleashing employees' natural creative potential at all levels of the organization.

> In fact, about 75 percent of ideas that result in better products or services for companies come from front-line workers. When management finds ways to harness that creativity, firms reap benefits.
> —*Alan Robinson*, Corporate Creativity: How Innovation and Improvement Actually Happen, *San Francisco: Berrett-Koehler, 1997*

Leading for Innovation: Engaging the Team in the Innovation Process

Hnedak Bobo Design Group is Memphis's largest architecture firm and a top 10 leader in the national hospitality and entertainment industry. The firm has received more than 200 design and industry awards for its innovative work. During a recent lunch, Kirk Bobo, cofounder and principal of Hnedak Bobo, shared his experience in unleashing personal and team creativity.

> "Every month I hold an open forum. The meeting is open to everyone in the company with one condition. The person attending should have a question, about anything we're doing, or an idea to share with others in the meeting.
>
> "The meeting has proven to be very useful to me personally. I always leave these meetings with

more ideas that have at times helped me in developing creative solutions to projects we are working on. I travel a lot, so don't get as much time as I'd like to just meet and talk with people in the office. The open forum provides an opportunity for me to meet and listen to their ideas. And it provides access for everyone in the group to ask questions and share their ideas with me. The forum makes people feel not only good individually but also part of a team working together to develop creative solutions to clients' needs."

The two terms for unleashing creativity are *why* and *what if*. Kirk's meeting is an excellent real-world example of using these simple and powerful words.

> To raise new questions (why), new possibilities (what ifs), to regard old questions from a new angle, requires creative imagination and marks real advances in science.
>
> —*Albert Einstein and L. Infield*

GAINING ACCEPTANCE OF CREATIVE IDEAS

I was asked by a financial services company to help unleash creativity and innovation in the organization. What I found during this consulting assignment was that the organization had lots of ideas but the ideas did not move forward because people were having difficulty gaining acceptance for their creative ideas. Gaining acceptance requires certain communication and interpersonal skills. People need help in learning these skills. It is leader's responsibility to provide the necessary training and coaching to help people on the team develop these skills.

> If you want to make enemies,
> try to change something.
> —*Woodrow Wilson*

Even though intellectually people understand that to grow and compete in the global economy the enterprise must change, at a personal level, for one or more of the following reasons, the change feels uncomfortable.

1. Different view of the world—genuine concern about how the idea will impact their areas/lives.

2. Discomfort at an emotional level—fear of the unknown. If a person fears failure, he won't take the risks involved in starting new projects and experimenting with new ways of doing things and will block his and other's capabilities for developing and implementing innovative ideas.

3. Vested interest in maintaining the status quo.

4. Internal dialogue—"I should've come up with this idea"—and ego in play.

To Gain Acceptance, All of the Above (Human) Concerns Must Be Addressed

In fact, instead of just acceptance, we want wholehearted acceptance, because then people are fully committed to a successful implementation. We've got to appeal to the whole person—the head and the heart.

The most potent way to win over people is to accept that they have legitimate concerns; that triggers an instinct to reciprocate. People can understand the analysis and perceive the projected cost savings but if they don't *feel* that the presenter fully appreciates their situation, they won't accept the idea.

When people feel understood and appreciated, it changes their feelings about the issue from negative to positive. It also transforms their feelings about the person presenting the idea.

A Proven Communication Model for Gaining Acceptance

- *Expect and respect different perspectives.* The people who will be affected by the change you are proposing have different perspectives on the situation based on their knowledge, experience, interests, and areas of responsibilities. Those perspectives must be respected. Once the mind is prepared to hear different perspectives then it does not become defensive.

- *Listen* to understand versus listening to respond. The deepest human need is "I matter." That means my ideas matter. When others listen to my ideas, I feel valued. Even though people may understand the general need for the change, they will probably feel uncomfortable about it. Those feelings need to be acknowledged and recognized. Validate their feelings by listening to understand versus listening to respond.

- *Speak* their language. Every function and department has its own vocabulary, priorities, knowledge, and experience base. You need to incorporate the function's language while presenting how your idea will benefit that group, how it will make their lives easier, and how it will help them achieve their goals.

    Use business instead of functional language. When you're in the trenches or playing a highly specialized or technical role, it's easy to fall into the trap of using technical or functional language in selling your ideas to senior management. Avoid that at all costs. Instead speak their language and explain how your ideas will help them reduce costs, increase revenue, and improve the company's value proposition by enhancing the customer experience.

- *Expand* ownership. By engaging people who have concerns or reservations about the change you are proposing, in exploring creative solutions to the concerns raised you are expanding ownership.

SUCCESSFUL IMPLEMENTATION

The acronym for the four skills in the model just discussed is *ELSE*. In Webster's dictionary the meaning is other (other than you); besides (you); in addition (to you).

Ask yourself who *else* you must have on the team to ensure successful development and implementation of your idea?

REVIEW IN ADVANCE THE IDEA/PROPOSAL ONE-ON-ONE WITH KEY PEOPLE

People want to be included and don't like being surprised or blind-sided. By discussing the idea in person privately with each of the key people before you raise it in a meeting, you're communicating that you value each person and his or her suggestions. By this simple act you've turned your idea into a joint venture and built a stronger case.

If for some reason you cannot discuss your idea in person and have to share it in a memo, including *draft* on it will convey to the person that your proposal is a work in process and that you're soliciting ideas to improve it. Make that explicit in the body of the proposal itself.

Build relationships with peers, for example, by scheduling lunches with them regularly. Personal relationships create comfort levels, making people more open to new ideas from others. It's human nature: The more shared experiences you have, the greater the comfort level. Lunch conversations about personal interests, hobbies, sports, and families pave the way for other conversations about work and ways of making it better. When I look back at my time at FedEx, these lunches played a big part in my enjoying a successful career. Relationships, more than information, determine how ideas get accepted and successfully implemented.

Your ultimate goal is not just acceptance but successful implementation of the idea. These people will play a key role in implementation. By learning and using people skills geared toward *gaining acceptance*, you are expanding ownership of the change idea as well and thus setting the stage for successful implementation.

Leading for innovation requires active involvement and support on leaders' part to help people develop and unleash their natural creative and innovation potential. Through their day-to-day behavior and attitude, leaders set an example for others to follow.

LOOKING OUT THE WINDOW AND TAKING ACTION TO STAY ONE STEP AHEAD OF THE COMPETITION

The process for sustained enterprise growth is to continuously look out the window to identify what changes are taking place in the larger business environment and then make creative changes internally to take advantage of the opportunities presented by the external changes.

We saw the mobile revolution early and we made a
big bet across the entire company. We saw that
mobile was an important factor for our customers.
It was becoming the central control device in their
lives. We didn't worry if it cannibalized our
existing business, because we knew it was what
our customers wanted.

—*John Donahoe, CEO, eBay, quoted by James B. Stewart
in the* New York Times, *July, 28, 2012*

The next section discusses two unleashing-innovation
lessons that are keys to building and sustaining an
innovation culture.

PART V

Two *Leading for Innovation* Lessons from Nature for Engaging Your Team in the Innovation Process

Many companies have succeeded in making everyone responsible for quality. We're going to have to do the same for innovation.

—Gary Hamel, Author and International Strategy Consultant, *Fortune*, April 2, 2001

The P&G five or six years ago depended on 8,000 scientists and engineers for the vast majority of innovation. The P&G

we're trying to unleash today asks all
100,000-plus of us to be innovators.
—A.G. Lafley, CEO, P&G, *Fortune*,
Special: CEOs on Innovation

LEADING FOR INNOVATION

Lesson 8: Tap into Strengths

Regardless of your role within the organization,
it is my job to make sure that you feel empowered
to lead from your seat. This is about recognizing
that you can influence change and outcomes, and
we all have to do that for us to be truly innovative,
to deliver on our mission to have breakthroughs.

—*Terri Ludwig, President and CEO, Enterprise
Community Partners, interviewed by Adam Bryant,*
New York Times, *August 21, 2011*

Lesson 9: Promote Diversity of Thought

I want my managers to listen and respond
to their employees' perceptions, not ignore them.
Managers have to be open to accepting any kind
of initiation. When they deny there's an issue
and reflexively defend the status quo, it creates
misery for people.

—*Dick Costolo, CEO, Twitter,* Bloomberg Businessweek,
April 15–April 21, 2013

Leading for Innovation Lesson 8: Tap into Strengths /

WHAT'S REVEALED IN NATURE: Different trees produce different fruits and have different needs.

TEACHES US: Tap into people's strengths and treat them how they want to be treated (the Platinum Rule).

Leading teams at both RCA and FedEx I discovered that on every team there are people who are:

- Good at generating ideas by asking *what if?*
- Good at accepting and developing the raw ideas.
- Good at implementing the developed ideas.

The role of the team leader is to identify and tap into each team member's strength and to tell that person that he or she is playing an equally important role in the innovation process. People have a psychological need to make a difference, and they want to be recognized when they do.

> Outstanding leaders go out of the way to boost the self-esteem of their personnel. If people believe in themselves, it's amazing what they can accomplish.
> —*Sam Walton, founder of Walmart*

LEADING FOR INNOVATION LESSON 8:
TAP INTO STRENGTHS
What's Revealed in Nature

Different trees produce different fruits and have different needs.

CREATIVITY LESSON

Tap into people's strengths and treat them how they want to be treated (the Platinum Rule).

See this photo in color at www.innovationculture.com.

Leading for Innovation Lesson 8: Tap into Strengths

Applying the Lesson

Larry Papasan started his career at Memphis Light Gas and Water as a junior engineer in 1963. He worked there for 28 years, the last eight as the president. He was recruited by Smith & Nephew to lead their orthopedics division as president in 1991. The division's annual sales in 1991 were $250 million. When Larry left Smith & Nephew in 2002, the sales had grown to $750 million.

Under Larry's leadership Smith & Nephew introduced several industry-leading innovations, the most notable being a patented oxidized zirconium knee implant. The key feature of this technology was reducing the wear between components, thus substantially increasing the life of the implant. The other important innovation was reducing the surgery preparation time from up to 2 hours to 30 minutes.

In addition to being an active community leader, Larry is sought after to serve on the board of start-ups and established companies. He serves on the boards of 10 for-profit companies and six nonprofits.

Innovation Is a Team Sport, and You're the Coach

Larry told the hiring manager at Smith & Nephew that he did not have technical knowledge of the orthopedics implant business. The recruiter told him they were pursuing him because of his strong people leadership and planning skills.

Both Larry and I are big sports fans, and we often talk about the local teams. He shared that on a winning team, the coach uses the players in positions that best use their natural talents. The coach also ensures that players on the team clearly understand that every win is a result of the cumulative effort of all players and that each player plays an equally important role. The innovation process—generation, acceptance, development, and successful implementation of innovative ideas—requires active collaboration of all involved departments. Innovation is a team sport. A business leader is the coach of the team he or she is leading.

Create Creative Tension by Setting Stretch Goals

Leading for innovation responsibilities include creating the right conditions for people to innovate. At the beginning of each fiscal year, Larry called the management team together to compare Smith & Nephew against the best in the industry. After the discussion he would set measurable, specific goals to stretch each manager. For leadership positions he looked for individuals who could make big improvements and achieve their stretch goals.

> We believe in big bets, and in high-risk and high-reward projects such as driverless cars and Android. By encouraging people to think bigger we often achieve far more than what we initially imagine.
>
> —*David Lawee, Vice President for Corporate Development at Google*, New York Times, *March 18, 2012*

Help Develop Right-Brain Imaginative Thinking

Innovation is both an art and science. We need both sides of the brain: the right side (imaginative and feeling) and the left side (rational and analytical). Innovation is a three-step process that includes generation, acceptance, and implementation of new creative ideas.

The first step, generation, starts in the imaginative right brain. The acceptance/development of the raw creative idea and successful implementation involves both the left and the right brain.

Larry regularly took the team off-site to participate in activities that stimulated managers' imaginations. One such activity was using play dough to create something that they probably had not dreamed of building: a piece of art. In another meeting at the Winter Olympics site in Calgary, Canada, he invited surgeons to join the management team. From that meeting they came back with new designs for several of their products.

> We are trying to set this up as a continuously
> learning organization. My role is creating
> that learning atmosphere.
>
> —*Reed Hastings, CEO, Netflix*, Bloomberg Businessweek,
> *May 13, 2013*

Ask and Internalize: What's the Most Important Contribution I Can Make?

When people move into management, they have three sets of responsibilities: technical/operational, managerial, and leadership. The most value-added one is people leadership, that is, the ability to inspire people on their team to get actively involved in the innovation process.

As a member of the FedEx Leadership Institute, I facilitated leadership development classes for frontline managers, senior managers, and managing directors. We devoted significant time to helping the participants internalize this message.

People are promoted into management because they were excellent as individual contributors. The human tendency is to stay in one's comfort zone. So even after becoming managers, they spend most of their time solving technical problems as individual contributors.

> GE is a "We Company," not a "Me Company."
> We want people who listen more than they talk.
> We want leaders who build teams.
> —*Jeff Immelt, GE 2011 Annual Report*

Treat People How They Want to Be Treated

We have all heard of the Golden Rule: Treat people like you want to be treated. Now there is the so-called Platinum Rule: Treat people how *they* want to be treated. Being an effective leader means finding what motivates each employee and using that information to inspire them to be actively engaged in the innovation process. This is the only way organizations can continuously design and deliver products and services that are superior to those of their competition.

If your colleagues believe that you respect and trust
their judgment, they'll pay you the compliment
of telling you what they really think. So remember:
Trust and candor travel together.

—*Ken Powell, CEO, General Mills*, Fortune, *May 4, 2009*

Tap into Strengths: Proven Ideas

- Innovation is a team sport, and you're the coach.

- Create creative tension by setting stretch goals.

- Help develop right-brain imaginative thinking.

- Ask and internalize: What's the most important contribution I can make?

- Treat people how they want to be treated.

LEADING FOR INNOVATION LESSON 9: PROMOTE DIVERSITY OF THOUGHT

WHAT'S REVEALED IN NATURE: Nature loves diversity because it increases the likelihood that species will be able to adapt to different and changing conditions.

TEACHES US: Promote diversity of thought and increase the company's ability to adapt to changing conditions.

Creative ideas germinate when people with different perspectives work together on the same problem. Earlier we discussed that creativity is the process of connecting dots in imaginative ways. When individuals express their ideas, they create more dots—including more diverse ones—available for the group to connect. What does it take to express new ideas?

- Belief that the leader wants new ideas from everyone
- Formal and informal ways to express new ideas
- Belief that the leader will take the expressed ideas seriously
- Belief that one will get credit for new ideas and perhaps a reward

Innovation leaders create and reinforce these beliefs by their day-to-day behaviors.

Leading for Innovation Lesson 9: Promote Diversity of Thought
What's Revealed in Nature

Nature loves diversity because it increases the likelihood that species will be able to adapt to different and changing conditions

Teaches Us

Promote diversity of thought and increase the company's ability to adapt to changing conditions.

See this photo in color at www.innovationculture.com.

LEADING FOR INNOVATION LESSON 9: PROMOTE DIVERSITY AND ADAPTABILITY

Applying the Lesson

Phaneesh Murthy was worldwide head of sales and marketing for Infosys, one of the world leaders in consulting, technology, and outsourcing, from 1995 until 2002. During that time, sales at Infosys increased from $2 million to $700 million. In 2003 he founded Quintant, with a unique global service model. Quintant was acquired by iGATE in 2003, and Phaneesh went on to become the chief executive officer (CEO) of iGATE Global, the Indian subsidiary of iGATE in 2003 and the CEO of iGATE corporation in 2008. In 2012, iGATE had revenue of more than $1 billion and 25,000 employees. I had a chance to interview Phaneesh to learn about his leadership in growing the enterprise.

Q: How did you achieve phenomenal sales growth from $2 million to $700 million?

PM: First, I got really motivated when people said that we'd never succeed. I thrive on that kind of challenge and work really hard to prove people wrong. Second, I had complete trust in our capabilities to deliver a superior customer value at a more economical price. Finally, achieving this phenomenal growth was a team effort. I built a team of "hungry tigers," what I call people who are super-enthusiastic.

My experience has been that people are most enthusiastic at the start of their careers, so we recruited graduates from leading schools. I knew firsthand that it is the sales people who are standing in front of the customers, so I gave them a high degree of empowerment and an incredible amount of organizational support. Selling is essentially building relationships. We built these mutually trusting relationships one customer at a time.

Q: What makes iGATE different from other similar businesses?

PM: The big differentiation is our innovative "Business Outcome" service delivery model. iGATE's industry-first model enables clients to pay only for outcomes and not for the time and materials that go into achieving those outcomes. This ensures we are fully aligned to our clients' goals, meet their business objectives and share the involved risks. This, in essence, is a "partnership model."

The other innovation that differentiates us from the competition is our iTOPS—integrated technology and operations—model. With iTOPS we help clients deliver services using technology and intellectual property instead of by increasing headcount. Using this model we are successfully assisting more than 30 insurance companies in policy administration and claims management. Clients pay only when the agreed outcome is achieved. We get paid per policy and per claim.

Q: How do you promote diversity of thought to develop innovative solutions for your clients?

PM: Three of our core values are innovation, passion, and respect for an individual. We hire and promote based on these values. The key component of respect for an individual is listening to his or her ideas. At every level of the organization it is expected that managers actively seek and listen to people's ideas. Our "Business Outcome" model requires that we tap into the creativity of every team member to develop innovative solutions for improving our clients' core processes and profitably delivering our services.

To ensure diversity of thought, we hire people from diverse backgrounds, not just software programmers. For example, we hire people with industrial automation backgrounds, user experience, and others. Every client service team consists of people from various fields.

We have multiple awards to encourage creativity and innovation, a pat-on-the-back for "Small Step Innovation," which are ideas that improve a process step, and a CEO award for larger impact innovation.

Any time you make an accomplishment visible,
people take notice and are inspired to achieve.

—*Dorothy Bunach, Director of NorTech, Continental,*
March 2002

Q: I saw in *Forbes* magazine recently that in the iGATE-
sponsored charity golf tournament last month, you
and your partner won the first place. How did you
do that?

PM: I enjoy playing golf but am not a great golfer by
any stretch. You just have to know how to pick
the right partner.

Phaneesh Murthy's skill in picking the right people
for the job, people who complement his strengths and
weaknesses, apparently pays off on the golf course, as well as
in business.

Chances are, members of your team have good ideas
that would help them achieve better results. As a team
leader, your responsibility is to help them express those ideas
publicly so that others can build on them to create innovative
business solutions.

If you have an apple and I have an apple
and we exchange apples, then you and I will
still each have one apple. But if you have an idea
and I have an idea and we exchange these ideas,
then each of us will have two ideas.

—*George Bernard Shaw*

Actively Seek Ideas from Others

Dale Whitehurst was head of RCA Music Service in Indianapolis and my boss when I worked there. I noticed in staff meetings that whenever an issue pertaining to a specific department would come up, he would draw everyone into the conversation, including the people from departments not directly involved. He would go around the room and ask each person for his or her thoughts. This allowed for different perspectives to surface. He always shared his thoughts at the end so as not to influence others' thinking. I've been in other meetings where the boss shared his thoughts at the start and everyone else just followed the direction set by the boss.

> I learned a lot [at the Advanced Management
> Program at the Harvard Business School,]
> and one of the things I learned is that there
> are always ideas out there that you don't know
> anything about. The more senior I got over time,
> the more I tried to seek those areas of diverse
> opinion to incorporate into my own thinking
> in making decisions.

—*Admiral Mike Mullen, Chairman of the Joint Chiefs, 2007–2011, interviewed by Geoffrey Colvin*, Fortune, *May 21, 2012*

Use Cross-Functional Teams

During my first 10 years at FedEx, I led the materials and resource planning (MRRP) group. MRRP was responsible for ensuring that the materials needed to run FedEx were available at the right place and at the right time, including airbills, an important five-part document required for shipping with FedEx.

In the early days, new products and services were introduced quite frequently. That resulted in modifying the five-part airbill constantly. Every time the airbill was changed and a new one introduced, the old airbill inventory had to be written off. Eventually, this cost of the write-off was approaching six figures.

A cross-functional team was formed, consisting of representatives from marketing, materials planning, procurement, the management information system group, and the airbill vendors, and given the task to minimize inventory write-offs.

Inventory levels are driven by several variables, the two key ones being the lead time and the variability of demand. Although the variability in demand created the need for safety stocks, the ideal situation would be 100 percent accurate forecasts and the shortest possible lead time. At that time, the lead time (elapsed time from the receipt of order to delivery to FedEx) from the vendors was eight weeks because of the time it took to get the different color papers used in the airbills from the paper mills.

The team set a goal of reducing the lead time to two weeks by adopting just-in-time inventory management practices being used in the manufacturing sector at that time.

Each team member was asked to share in detail his or her part of the total business process, thus making all the dots visible to every team member.

This total process visibility allowed the team to play what if, that is, to connect dots in imaginative ways and develop a new process that not only met but exceeded the goal. Signing a yearly contract and providing the vendors a rolling forecast for the next 12-month period, updated monthly, were key features of the new process. This allowed vendors to order and stock the different color papers from the paper mills. With unprinted paper on hand, the lead time for delivery of finished airbills to FedEx was reduced from eight weeks to two weeks, allowing significant reduction in the inventory write-offs.

> I have a weekly meeting with the inglorious
> title, discussion group, which has no agenda
> other than to bring ideas to the table.
> —*Amy Gutmann, President, University of Pennsylvania,*
> *interviewed by Adam Bryant*, New York Times, *June 18, 2011*

Watch Out for the Internal Dialogue That Says, "I Have the Right Answer"

As soon as the mind hears, "I have the right answer," it gets the signal that no more information is needed to solve the problem and it stops listening. The top psychological need for a person with an idea is to feel listened to. Once the word gets around that the boss is not receptive to new ideas, people on the team stop sharing their ideas.

If you act like a know-it-all, then no one will tell you anything. If you say you don't know, people come forward and want to tell you. People like to give advice and help.

—*Eileen Fisher, Founder and CEO of Eileen Fisher, Inc.*

Listening to Understand versus Listening to Respond

When people are talking, we're usually thinking about how we're going to respond rather than trying to understand them fully.

Q. Are there areas you want to improve as a leader?
A. My brain races too much, so even if I've listened to everything somebody said, unless you show that you've digested it, people don't think they're being well heard. . . . And so, if you really want to get the best out of people you have to really hear them and they have to feel like they've been really heard. So I've got to learn to slow down and improve in that dimension.

—*Steve Ballmer, CEO, Microsoft, interviewed by Adam Bryant,* New York Times, *May 17, 2009*

Let Appreciation Flow from the Heart

Employees have a need to be recognized for the quality and creativity of their work. A plaque, a letter, a pin, a cup, or a check are great and are appreciated, but recognition means much more if it comes from the presenter's heart. A smile, a kind word, a handwritten note, an honest compliment—all connect at the heart level.

> As we look ahead into the next century, leaders will be those who empower others.
> —*Bill Gates, cofounder, Microsoft*

Promote Diversity of Thought: Proven Ideas

- Actively seek ideas from others.
- Use cross-functional teams.
- Watch out for the internal dialogue that says, "I have the right answer."
- Listen to understand versus listening to respond.
- Let appreciation flow from the heart.

CLOSING THOUGHTS
MINT IN ACTION

FRED SMITH'S IDEA + EMPLOYEES' CREATIVITY = GLOBAL ICON

Fred Smith has single-handedly changed the way global business functions. He has achieved this transformation not because he happened to be in the right place at the right time, or because he had access to a new groundbreaking technology, but because he had a vision of how to combine existing technologies and develop new processes to realize new possibilities.

—Strategy & Leadership, *September/October 1997*

Yes, Fred Smith had the original idea for starting FedEx, but it was the creativity and commitment of employees at all levels of the organization that turned it into a globally successful business. The business growth and the promotion from within policy have allowed thousands of people to enjoy successful and rewarding careers.

The following are just some of the industry-changing innovations that were imagined and successfully implemented by employees. It is very important to note that all of them were conceived and implemented in the 1970s and 1980s, when technology was very primitive compared with today.

FedEx was:

- The first express company to install electronic communication systems in delivery vans.
- The first company to introduce an on-time delivery guarantee.
- The first company to develop handheld scanners.
- The first company to offer online tracking.

Let's question each other, our ideas, and potential scenarios. Questioning and planning will help us create a better FedEx; it will help us avoid major mistakes.

—*Alan Graf, CFO, FedEx*

MANAGEMENT PREFERS "WE CAN" PEOPLE

It was a privilege for me to work with and learn from Fred Smith, founder and chief executive officer (CEO), and Jim Barksdale, chief operating officer (COO), about how to lead for growth and innovation. I joined FedEx as manager of materials planning and two years later was promoted to the position of senior manager of materials and warehouse planning.

Four years later I was being considered for another promotion: managing director of materials and resource planning. In FedEx's early days, if you were up for a promotion to the managing director level, you had to meet with Fred Smith and Jim Barksdale to get their approval. Jim started the meeting by congratulating me on being a finalist for the position and inquired about my background before FedEx and my experience working at FedEx.

He said, "Madan, you are doing a good job as a senior manager and I'm sure you'll do a great job in the managing director position. You know we're in the middle of double-digit growth domestically and starting to expand internationally. This will require successful execution of our growth strategy by all departments in the company. Sharp people like you can come up with many good and valid reasons as to why a particular strategic change initiative won't work.

"The people I'm looking for to be on my team will say, 'Yes, we can successfully execute this change initiative. Here are the issues that must to be addressed and here are our ideas for addressing them.' I don't want us to ignore the issues. I want you to bring those to my attention. But along with the identification of the problems I want you to engage your team in coming up with creative solutions."

With this informal conversation, Jim set the expectation of leading for innovation. See Lessons 8 (Tap into Strengths) and 9 (Promote Diversity of Thought).

I was facilitating a half-day Leading for Innovation workshop for leaders of nonprofit organizations, when Mary McDonald, superintendent of Catholic schools in Memphis, shared with the class a quote reflecting similar sentiment: The person who says it cannot be done should not interrupt the person who is doing it.

SAARINEN: LEAVING A RICH LEGACY THROUGH CREATIVITY IN ARCHITECTURE

The following story illustrates well how nature's inspiration, combined with a vision greatly broadened as a result of living in different parts of the world, led to an extraordinary design career. The inspiration for this story came while enjoying a glass of red wine on the balcony of Holland America's ship *Eurodam*. To set the scene: The ship is cruising the Baltics. It's around 10 PM; a beautiful orange glow is on the horizon as the sun is getting ready to set. Seagulls are swooping down to catch fish, and the slapping of waves against the ship is creating a pleasant, rhythmic sound.

During the day the ship is docked at Helsinki, and the guided tour of the city took us to the houses of three young architects: Eliel Saarinen, Herman Gesellius, and Armas Lindgren. Upon graduation they opened their joint architectural office in Helsinki and were commissioned to design the Finnish pavilion for the Paris World Exhibition in 1900. Their successful design brought them international recognition and new commissions.

In 1901 the three architects decided to move away from Helsinki to a 40-acre site by Lake Hvittrask ("white lake" in old Swedish) at Kirkkonummi, where each architect designed his own house. The Saarinen home is a museum today. The house and the garden are surrounded by beautiful nature, a perfect setting for inspiration and creative thinking.

After winning the second prize in the *Chicago Tribune* Tower Competition in 1922, Saarinen decided to move to the United States with his family. Eliel Saarinen and his son Eero designed many notable projects in the United States, including the TWA Terminal at JFK International Airport and the Gateway Arch in St. Louis, Missouri.

EASING BRAIN FATIGUE WITH A WALK IN THE PARK

Scientists have known for some time that the human brain's ability to stay calm and focused is limited and can be overwhelmed by the constant noise and hectic, jangling demands of city living, sometimes resulting in a condition informally known as brain fatigue.

With brain fatigue, you are easily distracted, forgetful and mentally flighty—or, in other words me. But an innovative study from Scotland suggests that you can ease brain fatigue simply by strolling through a leafy park. The idea that visiting green spaces like parks or tree-filled plazas lessens stress and improves concentration is not new.

—*Gretchen Reynolds*, New York Times, *March 27, 2013*

IN MOTHER NATURE'S LAP
WE EXPERIENCE PEACE,
A SENSE OF AWE,
AND THE FREEDOM TO
PLAY AND IMAGINE.

It is a common misconception that Newton was hit on the head by an apple at his family home in Lincolnshire in the UK. Instead, the much touted moment happened while watching fruit fall to the ground. He did, however, credit the fresh air and beauty of the orchard for clearing his mind ahead of unearthing the laws of gravity.

—*Anna Whitehouse*, KLM *magazine*, Holland Herald, *July 2012*

Everyone is creative, including you—especially you. Don't let anybody tell you otherwise, including yourself. We're all blessed with some natural aptitude reflected in what we enjoy doing—our passions. What I've experienced is that expressing talents in one part of life carries over to the other parts, thus making life's journey a creative and joyous one.

Ideas are the most powerful things in the world, far more powerful than money. Best of all, there are no barriers to having great ideas and thinking big. Whether rich or poor, privileged or disadvantaged, everybody is capable of changing their lives and the lives of others by thinking big. It takes imagination, courage, and the will to work hard. Don't listen to the knockers and the critics, the naysayers and the negativity. To my knowledge nobody ever built a monument to a critic. They come and go but big ideas last forever.

—*Clive Palmer, Chairman and Founder of Mineralogy*, Bloomberg Businessweek, *April 15, 2013*

Keep growing your knowledge base (adding more dots) and imaginatively connecting these dots to develop and unleash your natural creative potential. Imagination grows by the exercise of imagination. Creative problem solving skill—what if thinking—grows by the exercise of asking *what if?* Ideas happen in conversations. The mind has this unique capability to connect dots across brains. Trust yourself and your mind's creative thinking process.

> There is something magical about sharing meals. There is something magical spending the time together, about noodling on ideas.
> —*Patrick Pichette, Google's Chief Financial Officer*, Financial Times, *February 28, 2013*

NOTHING HAPPENS IN THE BUSINESS WORLD WITHOUT A PROCESS

As discussed earlier innovation involves generation, acceptance, and implementation of creative ideas that enhance the customer value proposition. Innovative enterprises have processes that actively engage employees in the innovation process, either in generating ideas, in developing the ideas, or in implementing the ideas. FedEx's long-range planning process, which I participated in for nine years, engaged people from all operating and planning departments to explore and implement strategic what ifs.

> First, we break the company—which has 8,000
> employees—into four- to six-person teams. They
> observe the customers. They watch someone in a
> coffee shop, they watch someone in a florist
> shop . . . they look for big problems that are get-
> ting in their way. Then they come back to the office
> and come up with at least seven different ways to
> solve the problem.
>
> —*Brad Smith, CEO, Intuit*

CAREER GROWTH AND ENTERPRISE GROWTH GO TOGETHER

Many employees, in addition to myself, were able to enjoy successful careers because of FedEx's phenomenal growth and expansion. Employees at all levels of the organization helped FedEx develop and successfully execute its domestic and international growth strategies. This expansion in turn presented career growth opportunities for people across the enterprise.

Similarly, creativity and innovation are needed in every sector of the economy. In today's highly competitive economy, creative ideas are required and expected in every area at every step of the way, not just in the research and development department.

I intentionally selected a wide range of people to interview for this book, covering a number of fields—medicine, engineering, technology, services, manufacturing, architecture, education, and sports. The sizes of the organization they work in range from $25 million to $45 billion in annual revenue. They represent both for-profit and the nonprofit sectors.

None of the individuals I interviewed started at the top. Like you and me they all started their careers at the entry level. By continuously growing knowledge, trusting themselves, and solving problems creatively—by exploring what ifs before locking into how to—they helped their organizations grow and subsequently moved up the career ladder.

All of the individuals interviewed for this book—Kirk Bobo, Dr. Bhaskar Rao, Larry Papasan, Rob Carter, Jay Myers, Gayle Rose, Jenny Koltnow, Don Hutson, Ram Ramadorai, Carol Roberts, Becky Wilson, Phaneesh Murthy, and Adrian Bejan—illustrate this principle: *When you grow, the enterprise grows. When the enterprise grows, it presents opportunities for individuals with initiative to tackle challenges, make bigger contributions, and enjoy a rewarding, fulfilling career.* These are the two mutually reinforcing processes.

In the May 20, 2013, *Harvard Business Review Blog* "The Graduation Advice We Wish We'd Been Given," Dorie Clark, a strategy consultant who has worked with clients including Google, Yale University, and the National Park Service commented, "You need to hone a skill no one teaches you in college, and few people in the workforce understand: the ability to identify problems no one has explicitly articulated, and then solve them." From personal experience, this is a valuable skill not just when you start your career but throughout it.

Curiosity precedes creativity. Constantly question the assumptions behind the existing business models, product designs, and business processes. These assumptions may have been valid 5, 10 years ago when the process or product was initially designed, but the world and technology have changed significantly since then. This process will lead you to propose creative solutions and therefore position you for the next promotion.

The fruits of creative ideas (what ifs) have always fallen from the tree of curiosity.

Where creativity and innovation are nurtured, people and organizations blossom (realize their full potential.)

SUMMARY

Seven *Unleashing Creativity* Lessons

The Four Requirements for Creative Thinking (MINT)

More Dots (Expanded Knowledge Base)

Lesson 1: Grow Knowledge

Continually grow your knowledge base, a prerequisite for generating creative ideas.

Lesson 2: Be Persistent

Be persistent in developing your unique talents and nurturing your ideas.

Imagination (To Connect Dots)

Lesson 3: Trust Yourself

Trust that all the resources, including imagination, for germinating creative ideas are within you.

Lesson 4: Stay Calm

To make and see the imaginative new connections, the mind must be undisturbed.

Nominal Stress (Creative Tension)

Lesson 5: Take Risk (in expressing your ideas)

Take the risk inherent in setting innovation goals (creative tension) and expressing your imperfect ideas

Lesson 6: Minimize Negativity

Minimize internal and external negative influences that obstruct creative energy flow.

Time (To Think and Nurture Ideas)

Lesson 7: Unplug Your Devices

Schedule quiet time for creative thinking by turning off all electronic devices.

Two *Leading for Innovation* Lessons

Lesson 8: Tap into Strengths

Tap into people's strengths and treat them how they want to be treated (the Platinum Rule).

Lesson 9: Promote Diversity of Thought

Promote diversity of thought and increase the company's ability to adapt to changing conditions.

References

Bejan, Adrian, and J. Pedar Zane. *Design in Nature: How the Constructal Law Governs Evolution in Biology, Physics, Technology & Social Organizations.* New York: Doubleday, 2012.

Birla, Madan. *FedEx Delivers: How the World's Leading Shipping Company Keeps Innovating and Outperforming the Competition.* Hoboken, NJ: John Wiley & Sons, 2005.

Cameron, Julia. *The Creative Life: True Tales of Inspiration.* New York: Tarcher/Penguin, 2010.

Gerstner, Louis V., Jr. *Who Says Elephants Can't Dance? Inside IBM's Historic Turnaround.* New York: HarperCollins, 2002.

Godin, Seth. *Wisdom, Inc.: 26 Business Virtues That Turn Ordinary People into Extraordinary Leaders.* New York: HarperCollins, 1995.

Hamel, Gary. *Leading the Revolution: How to Thrive in Turbulent Times by Making Innovation a Way of Life.* New York: Plume, 2000.

Haskell, David George. *The Forest Unseen: A Year's Watch in Nature.* New York: Viking/Penguin, 2012.

Kanter, Rosabeth Moss. *The Change Masters: Innovation for Productivity in the American Corporation.* New York: Simon & Schuster, 1983.

Louv, Richard. *Last Child in the Woods, Saving Our Children from Nature Deficit Disorder*. New York: Workman Publishing, 2005.

Louv, Richard. *The Nature Principle: Human Restoration and the End of Nature Deficit Disorder*. Chapel Hill, NC: Algonquin Books, 2011.

Newton, James. *Uncommon Friends: Life with Thomas Edison, Henry Ford, Harvey Firestone, Alexis Carrel, & Charles Lindbergh*. Florida: Harcourt Brace, 1987.

Ray, Michael, and Rochelle Myers. *Creativity in Business*. New York: Doubleday, 1986.

Van Doren, Mark. *The Portable Emerson*. New York: Viking Press, 1974.

Wakefield, Dan. *Creating from the Spirit: Living Each Day as a Creative Act*. New York: Ballantine Books, 1996.

ACKNOWLEDGMENTS

First I want to thank Matt Holt, Shannon Vargo, Elana Schulman, and Lauren Freestone at John Wiley & Sons for their creative suggestions and excellent support. Sarah Bolton and Beverly Cruthirds deserve special thanks for not just editing but raising questions when the message was not coming through clearly.

I really appreciate Kirk Bobo, Dr. Bhaskar Rao, Larry Papasan, Rob Carter, Jay Myers, Gayle Rose, Jenny Koltnow, Don Hutson, Ram Ramadorai, Carol Roberts, Becky Wilson, Phaneesh Murthy, and Prof. Adrian Bejan for taking time from their busy schedules to share their work and life experiences.

My sincere thanks to the following for also taking time from their busy schedules to read chapter drafts and provide valuable feedback: Ed Hirsch, Becky Wilson, Kirk Bobo, Ben Buffington, Gayle Rose, and Brian and Deana Spangler.

I must thank Arun Kumtha, a very dear friend, for organizing our Sunday school group's annual outings to beautiful national parks, including Yellowstone, the Smokies, the Canadian Rockies, and state parks in Arkansas, Kentucky, and Tennessee. This ongoing communion with nature has played a big role in helping me learn nature's lessons.

Finally, I want to convey my deepest appreciation to Shashi, my life partner, for allowing me to spend hours at a time in the study working on this book.

ABOUT THE AUTHOR

Author (left) receiving his second Five Star Award, the highest recognition for Leadership Excellence at FedEx, from Fred Smith, Founder and CEO of FedEx.

Madan Birla is a veteran of the "hard" side of business. In his 22 years at FedEx, he worked closely with Fred Smith (founder and chief executive officer) and the senior management team in evaluating strategic what ifs.

His life experiences in two rich cultures, East and West, and his broad educational background have prepared him well to creatively meld ideas from engineering, business, psychology, and spirituality to develop comprehensive Leading for Innovation and Growth models.

He received his Master of Science in industrial engineering from the Illinois Institute of Technology (IIT) in Chicago, Illinois. After graduating from IIT, he joined RCA in Indianapolis. While in Indianapolis, he did graduate work in business at Butler University. After moving to Memphis to join FedEx, he received a Master of Science in counseling from the University of Memphis.

He is a regular speaker in executive education programs at Kellogg Management Institute, Northwestern, Tuck Business School, Dartmouth, American Management Association, the Conference Board, Indian School of Business, Indian Institute of Management, Singapore Institute of Management, and others.

His book *FedEx Delivers: How the World's Leading Shipping Company Keeps Innovating and Outperforming the Competition*, published by John Wiley & Sons, has been translated into Orthodox Chinese, Simplified Chinese, Russian, Spanish, Korean, Vietnamese, Thai, and other languages.

PRODUCTS AND SERVICES AVAILABLE

Madan Birla regularly speaks at companies, at business and professional groups' meetings, and on college campuses. He advises organizations and executives on how to unleash employee creativity and commitment to build a culture of innovation and superior performance.

To help reinforce the *Unleashing Creativity* and *Leading for Innovation* lessons, we have developed motivational posters, calendars, and other products. For more information on these products and services, please visit **www.innovationculture.com**.

INDEX